THREE-MARTINI
FAMILY VACATION

THE

THREE-MARTINI FAMILY VACATION

A Field Guide to Intrepid Parenting

by Christie Mellor

CHRONICLE BOOKS

SAN FRANCISCO

I would like to gratefully acknowledge the following people, without whose help this book would have been thin, dull, and probably unfinished:

Thanks to Richard Goldman, for the love, inspiration, and spaghetti; to my enthusiastic and agreeable editor, Jay Schaefer; to the stellar Leslie Daniels, giving agents everywhere a good name; to Micaela Heekin and the creative people at Chronicle Books who made this book look so good; and as always, to the ever-wonderful Jack Jensen. Thanks to Alicia Brandt, friend and provider of paper dolls; to Cyd Strittmatter and her personal tales of insanity; to great friends and fall guys Lisa and Phil Noyes; to the rambunctious and understanding Ladies of Book Group; to Wendy and Jane, the two best sisters a girl could have; to Wendy Goldman, friend and tonic; and special thanks to Dan Ratushny and Megan Shull, the nicest strangers in the whole wide world. Lastly, a big, wet thank-you kiss to the children and parents who unintentionally inspired me to write this book.

Library of Congress Cataloging-in-Publication Data available.

ISBN-10: 0-8118-5733-6
ISBN-13: 978-0-8118-5733-8

Manufactured in the United States.

Designed by Jay Peter Salvas
Artwork by Christie Mellor
Typesetting by Janis Reed

Distributed in Canada by Raincoast Books
9050 Shaughnessy Street
Vancouver, British Columbia V6P 6E5

10 9 8 7 6 5 4 3 2 1

Chronicle Books LLC
680 Second Street
San Francisco, California 94107

www.chroniclebooks.com

This book is dedicated
with much love
to my favorite Three-Martini gents,
Richard, Edison, and Atticus

· CONTENTS ·

⁻ HELPFUL HINTS & RECIPES ⁻

IN PRAISE OF
GETTING OUT OF THE HOUSE

RAISING CHILDREN CAN BE AN INCREDIBLY TIME-CONSUMING, often thankless pursuit, and although it is not without its rewards, we certainly could all use a little more time for ourselves.

Sadly, it is not always possible to wander off by yourself, as society generally frowns on putting the children in the cupboard while you go out barhopping. Still, a reasonable grown-up simply has to get out of the house from time to time. We all need the occasional quick visit with an adult friend, a change of scenery, a meal made by someone else. Sometimes we *like* to bring our kids on an outing to a coffee shop or a foreign country; sometimes we have no choice but to bring them.

It's not that you don't adore cooking breakfasts and dinners and helping the youngsters with homework; it's not that you don't look forward every day to picking dried bits of food out of the carpet and waking up really, really early to make school lunches and tell your children to brush their teeth. And certainly listening to your five-year-old scream for forty-two minutes at the dentist yesterday was excellent fun.

(He found the toothpaste a teeny bit spicy!) But it could be time for a little getaway.

Trust me, there is never going to be the "perfect time" to go on a vacation, and if you wait for the ideal moment, you will be old and gray, and too finicky to want to travel anywhere you can't have your shredded wheat and regular "programs." Do not wait. Go now.

Traveling with children in tow can be challenging, but so can traveling with anybody who doesn't want to do exactly what you want to do exactly when you want to do it. It's annoying, but there you are. You could put a rucksack over your shoulder and abscond in the dead of night, leaving your broken-hearted family to pick up the shattered remnants of their lives without their mommy or daddy, or you could give it a try, and discover that "traveling" and "with children" don't have to be mutually exclusive.

As you've no doubt already discovered if you have children, we are on an adventure as soon as we leave the house in the morning: A stop at the market, a bus trip to the library, a short jaunt to our favorite wine store can all be thrilling experiences for a young child, and a treat for you too, if your favorite wine store is anything as good as mine. The simplest trip to the post office with your four-year-old can be an action-packed expedition, albeit one that will go a lot smoother if your pocket-sized companion knows not to race into traffic, eat off the linoleum, or play Nok Hockey with someone's packages.

It's important that your children learn how to negotiate their local landscape, and if you intend to let them loose on an unsuspecting public—whether at home or abroad—they should really know how to behave.

If your children have never been given the tools to know how to behave outside your house and out in the world, how will you ever be able to take them to Grandma's, to your friend's house, to a restaurant, or on an airplane?

Eventually you may want to take them somewhere that isn't Child-Friendly. Eventually you may tire of the primary colors, the slightly greasy tabletops, and the ubiquitous pizzas that are endemic to the Child-Friendly venue. Eventually you may just want to break out of the whole noisy, sticky Child-Friendly lifestyle and usher the family into the not always People-Friendly but nearly always interesting "Real World," where people are often judged by the volume of their whine.

I hope this book will help make that transition just a little easier. And in case you are planning that trip, I have included many other chapters that might help you, as a parent, encourage a little more autonomy in your child; by giving your child some tools for independence, perhaps you will learn to enjoy a little more independence yourself.

But get out of the house, won't you? You really don't need to see one more award-winning episode of that educational TV show, do you? You can reschedule your playgroup. The laundry can wait. It's time for a little adventure.

CHAPTER I

LET'S MEET AT THAT REALLY NOISY CAFÉ FULL OF BRATTY CHILDREN!

WHILE IT MAY BE TOO MUCH TO EXPECT A CHILD OF FOUR OR five to sit at a fine dining establishment without fidgeting or howling, there are many open-air cafés and child-friendly venues where Mom or Dad can sit down with a friend while their children crayon the paper place mats and drop their bread on the floor.

Obviously, if I should choose to avail myself of the local Chuck E. Cheese, I pretty much know what I am getting myself into, and in fact, should you ever find me in a Chuck E. Cheese you may assume I have gone insane, and you should alert the appropriate authorities. A casual coffeehouse, on the other hand, should theoretically be territory friendly to both child and adult. Coffeehouse habitués don't usually gather at their local spot in order to play tag, and should there be a few scattered strollers and mommies, one still expects to be able to find a quiet corner.

I have often found myself in such a place, however, and noticed more than a few noisy children who appear to have

the run of the place, and who seem to belong to nobody. I do not believe the management has rented these children for the afternoon in order to add a certain carefree charm to the atmosphere, and I can't believe that they have simply been abandoned by their parents, as tempting an option as that might be. Could these untamed youngsters be free-spirited orphan street urchins? Surely they belong to someone. Perhaps that woman over there, the one intently sipping her beverage and chatting with her friend, while averting her eyes from the two children engaged in the loud burping match under someone else's table.

I understand that you are tired, and need to talk to a fellow exhausted friend. I understand that you are thankful that your little one can finally blow off some of that seemingly endless reserve of energy, while you enjoy a foamy latte. But eventually we will figure out that you are the parent of the child who is shaking salt into the potted palm and throwing Cheerios. You think that if you don't make eye contact with your child or the other annoyed adults in the vicinity, we will all disappear. If you don't look at us, we will not exist, and you can pretend you're in a magical land of Sleeping In and Quiet Alone Time, where you can drink your coffee in peace.

Despite my seemingly judgmental attitude, I have been known, on occasion, to delight in the boundless enthusiasm of children. My delight might be keener, however, if the level of screaming was turned down just a notch, and I wasn't being jostled by the pint-sized human choo-choo train continuously circumnavigating my table at a harrowing pace. A little well-placed supervision would be so appreciated.

This does not mean venturing a meek "Honey, that's enough! Sweetie, stop, okay?" and then diving back into the conversation with your friend. It may require actually rising from your comfy perch, temporarily abandoning your friend and coffee, and physically bringing your child *back to the table with you*. At this juncture you might take a moment to explain to your child that it's okay if she has some fun, but that she still must be considerate of other people. "Consideration of others" might include not running around the table of that nice lady over there while screaming with an intensity that could curdle a soufflé. Because that nice lady over there might be taking notes for her next book about horrible children and their clueless parents.

Let's say your little darling is chasing birds at an outdoor café. The patient people at the surrounding tables, while charmed the first few times, become increasingly irritable the forty-ninth time your squealing child whizzes by their table. The birds don't look all that thrilled either. You may think it's difficult to read emotion on the faces of birds, but you can see it in their beady eyes. When they've had enough, they've had enough, and you had better hope your name isn't Tippi.

Perhaps you have heard this halfhearted refrain, or something like it, at one of your favorite outdoor venues:

"Don't chase the birds, honey!" says Mommy, without moving. "Sweetie, it's not nice to chase the birds!" she gently admonishes, as her three-year-old starts throwing rocks at the pigeons. "Honey!" she calls in a soothing, dulcet tone. "Don't be mean to the birdies!"

She continues her conversation, oblivious, as her active young ornithologist experiments with high-pitched sound, apparently in an attempt to break the tiny eardrums of his prey.

If this scenario sounds vaguely familiar, next time try corralling your child back to his chair, explaining that it is bad manners to irritate other people. Share with him the concept of "getting on one's nerves," discussing the possible origin of the expression. In addition, you might ask him if he'd appreciate being chased every time he was about to tuck into a nice pile of crumbs, reminding him that we must be considerate of our avian friends as well. A small cup of steamed milk might divert him for a short spell, and if all else fails, you might suggest that it's time to go home, because coffeehouses are civilized, grown-up places, and that you will come back to the nice coffeehouse when he is ready to behave like a civilized human being.

CHAPTER 2

WHEN MR. RIGHT IS YOUR
FIVE-YEAR-OLD

I WAS IN THE MIDDLE OF ONE OF THOSE RARE ADULT CON-versations at the house of a mommy friend when she suddenly announced that it was "too quiet." It's not as if she has a curious toddler who might get into mischief with the solvents under the sink; her child is nearly five years old. Nevertheless, she yelled out his name and took off in search of him. Her panic was caused by the fact that he hadn't called *her* name for five whole minutes, but her fears were allayed when he was found about ten feet away, miraculously playing on his own, having found something to do that didn't involve his mommy's full atten-tion. I would have thought that the sight of her son playing by himself would be a welcome relief to this mother. Alas, no; she had to check on him, he had to show her the flawless stack-ing job he'd done with the blocks, and the spell was broken. Her child once again became the center of attention.

It's not just the children who are glued to their mom-mies; it's often the mommies who seem incapable of letting their child simply be, even on those infrequent occasions when the child has actually found something to take his mind off his mother.

Some mommies are apparently under the impression that if they aren't zealously interacting with their children all day, every day, they are somehow being remiss in their maternal duties. Thus they bring their children everywhere: to restaurants, to grocery stores, to dinner parties, to grown-up cocktail parties, to the movies, and, every once in a while, to my house.

Some friends of ours, invited for cocktails and dinner, arrived with their five-year-old. Mommy had to get the little one settled, a pursuit that generally takes the entire evening, as a shrill squeal emanates from the depths of his little soul if Mommy should stray more than a few feet. This particular evening, she spent about half an hour with him, and then, astonishingly, he began to happily (and quietly!) join in a game with my children in the front room. It was a miracle not seen on previous visits: her child, seemingly oblivious to his mother's whereabouts, was actually playing, with no grown-ups lurking in the vicinity to watch him play.

I had wisely gone ahead and mixed cocktails for the adults, so I gestured silently for Mommy to follow the rest of us out to the back patio, where we could all, finally, have a grown-up visit. There we were, having stealthily made our way out the back door, the children playing contentedly in the front room, the grown-ups just taking that first sip of chilled cocktail, when Mommy suddenly exclaimed, "Oh! A bunny! I forgot you guys have a bunny!" upon which she immediately *started back toward the house,* exhorting her little one with a shrill "ELLIOT! ELLIOT, COME SEE THE BUNNY!" before I could tackle her to the ground and put a gag firmly in place.

I know the damn bunny is precious, and so is your little boy, but couldn't we possibly have postponed this magical meeting of child and bunny for, say, ten or twenty minutes? Allowing us to have a few uninterrupted sips of our beverages while exchanging a few adult pleasantries? Would that have been too much to ask?

It's sadly true that many parents inexplicably do not crave either martinis or time with their grown-up friends, but sometimes I think it's because their children have trained them too well. The bunny wasn't going anywhere, and certainly little Elliot would have been at the back door soon enough with his usual plaintive cry for Mommy and a squeal of delight as he set about tormenting our skittish woodland creature. When suddenly faced with a group of actual adults, Mommy's first instinct was to send for her favorite little buddy. I don't think it's because she doesn't like us; I think she's been hanging out with the under-five set for so long that she's out of practice interacting with adults.

Okay, maybe she just doesn't like us. But she could have pretended for one night, couldn't she?

I know many parents feel it is their job to be their child's constant playmate and companion; that time goes by too quickly, and those precious moments will be lost in the blink of an eye. But as virtuous as it may make you feel to be spending every waking moment as your child's caregiver, it is also your job to give your child the tools to be a self-sufficient and independent person.

A few years ago, as I recall the story, a nice Danish couple parked their stroller outside a New York City restaurant and popped inside to enjoy a meal. When it was discovered that they had actually left the baby *inside the stroller,* an uproar of epic proportions ensued. They had only had a few margaritas when the cops appeared on the scene, and the unsuspecting couple was promptly arrested for child abandonment, or something equally heinous.

A New York City sidewalk is perhaps not the optimum spot to leave one's infant unattended, and this may be an extreme measure to ensure a little grown-up time, but the basic idea is very civilized, and were it not for crowded streets and those few bothersome child abductions that take place once every few years, wouldn't it be just lovely to park one's child and slip into a warm café for some quiet time?

I know, I've said too much, and the bad-mommy police will be paying me a little visit soon. Now, I'm not suggesting that children should be ignored, or whisked away by nannies and kept in the east wing of the house until they're all grown up. But must we see them every minute of every day?

It is not wrong to adore your children with the white-hot passion of a thousand suns, and to want to love them up every second. But you might, in fact, *benefit* from a little break. And when you take that break, you might try letting your child have a little break, too. It will be good for him to get used to interacting with people other than his parents. You may not realize it, but he needs the practice. Really, he does. You can rejoin the lovefest rested and refreshed after a much-needed respite from each other.

Children need a certain amount of general supervision, but they don't need to be hovered over. Will your child be incapable of playing by himself because he has never been allowed to be without a constant playmate and companion? Will he be unable to function without his nose in an electronic gaming device or his eyes glued to the TV, because he doesn't know how to entertain himself? Go set up some blocks within earshot of your child, or maybe a little table with crayons and paper. Firmly sit your child down in front of these blocks and/ or crayons, while you get some things done. Your child may resist at first, but schedule a few minutes of "alone time" into each day, and then add more until it becomes routine. It may help your "together time" be that much more rewarding.

A Helpful Hint!

EVERYONE MAKES MISTAKES: A NOTE ON THE BUNNY

Y Y Y

SOME OF YOU MAY HAVE HEARD ME REMARK AT ONE TIME OR *another, "If I ever end up with a goddamn bunny, please just shoot me," but at this time I would like to ask you to not, in fact, shoot me. I may have spoken hastily. I may have spoken too soon, before I realized how prevalent is the possibility of accidentally acquiring bunnies. It's not as if I went out and procured this bunny; this bunny, more or less, wound up in our backyard. The bunny in question was first discovered in a sidewalk shrub by our neighbors who live across the street. They alerted us, and then mysteriously disappeared as soon as my children showed up. I didn't want the damn bunny to get run over by a car or eaten by a dog or anything, okay? Honestly, I'm not entirely without a heart. So we toss him a few carrots once in a while and he keeps the grass clipped, and sees to it that my tomatoes and cucumbers never grow to a size where we might get to actually eat them. Cute? Adorable! But if I ever end up with a goddamn hamster or guinea pig, then you absolutely have my permission to put me out of my misery.*

CHAPTER 3

YOUR ENDLESSLY FASCINATING CHILD

FINALLY, IT'S YOUR DAY TO GET TOGETHER WITH YOUR group of friends and their attendant strollers/babies. It's something you look forward to all week, a chance to sip coffee with a group of grown-ups for a change, have some much-needed adult conversation, and catch up with your pals. Perhaps talk some politics, or discuss a book you recently read. Or thought about reading. But you are tired, because you have been so busy chasing your toddler around the house. So you park the stroller, take a sip of your coffee, and start talking about how tired you are from chasing your toddler around the house. Then your friend takes a sip of her coffee and starts in on how she hasn't been getting any sleep, except that it's all worth it because her baby makes such funny faces, and look, I have vomit on my shirt, ha ha! And it suddenly dawns on you that you are spending your entire time with your adult friends discussing your children.

Now, it could be that you all love to get together for the sole purpose of sharing heartwarming and/or hilarious stories about your babies and toddlers; it could be that you all like nothing more than hearing the latest news regarding little Becca's teething, and how charming it was when Cameron landed his first poop in the potty—certainly that alone is cause for celebration of the highest order. Or it could be that your friends aren't all that interesting anyway, and just getting out of the house and having a cup of coffee is reward enough. If that is the case, then enjoy your coffee and your friends, and don't mind me.

But as a cautionary tale, I would like to mention a woman of my acquaintance who is prone to talking endlessly about her child; her child, by the way, who is no longer a new baby or an adorable toddler. Imagine running into this proud mama at school, and the grocery store, and at parties, and having to hear the ins and outs of her child's captivating life and personality over a period of twelve years, at forty minutes a pop, and then imagine how you might start plotting her slow death by poison, just as so many have done before you. Among our mutual friends, there is an unspoken rule: Never, *ever*, mention your own child around this woman, as it will only set her off, and once she's started it's difficult to bring her around to any topic of conversation that might be more engaging than the subject of her child. Even when you avoid mention of your own children, an innocent remark about the inclement weather might bring on a complete and detailed recounting of her child's latest sinus infection. Should you mention your garden, a moving monologue must be endured on how her son just refuses to eat root vegetables, with specific information on what he does eat, and how it affects his allergies. If you happen to debate, while discussing civic matters, whether or not that new stadium should be built downtown, a lengthy account of her youngster's Little League exploits will surely ensue.

In the not-so-distant past, such people would have been called "bores." Now they are called "mommies."

If you think you'd like to expand your group's conversational vistas just a little wider, I might suggest the following bylaws for your coffee klatch, as a way to raise the level of discourse.

1. The first person to talk about his/her child(ren) has to buy lattes for everyone.

2. The first member to wonder aloud whether it's "normal" for his/her fifteen-month-old to be speaking in complete sentences or reading aloud is banned for a month.

3. The first member to share the news that his/her baby is sleeping through the night is banned for three months.

4. If a member should somehow turn a discussion about, say, the skyrocketing national debt into a

monologue about his/her child, said member will be banned from the group, preferably to live in exile in a room full of colicky babies, along with the other banned members of the group who could not stop talking about their children.

5. The first member to start talking about the rigors of early education while his/her child is still horizontal in a stroller must write one hundred times "My child is only eighteen months old, which is too young to absorb serious academics. He needs to play and be a baby for several more years. Also, I am an idiot who now must buy overpriced coffees for everyone."

6. If you have bought lattes for everyone for more than two weeks in a row, you will be required to buy lunch for everyone.

7. If a mention of your child is relevant to the discussion, and/or you are bursting with news of your child that cannot wait, a signal must be given and the Group Stopwatch must be located. Three to five minutes should be adequate for you to share the news.

8. If you find that you are buying lunch for your friends every week, perhaps this group is not for you. You might seek out a slightly more child-friendly group, perhaps a nice Mommy & Me or Gymboree class, where you will finally be able to talk about your child to your heart's content.

CHAPTER 4

KRAZY MIXED-UP
UPSIDE-DOWN FAMILY

A CERTAIN MOMMY FRIEND OF MINE IS AT HER WITS' END because her fifteen-month-old has taken over the household. The grown-ups are still the ones who have to make the money, cook the meals, clean the house, and support everyone, but now they do all that with no discernible perks.

For instance, this happy family took all the chairs out of the dining room because their fifteen-month-old likes to climb. "She's a climber!" they say, as they sit down to dinner. As they sit down to dinner *on the floor*. Where they eat every meal. Now, if they'd suddenly decided to eat on the floor because of a resolve to cast off the trappings of Western civilization, or because it's a more enjoyable way to eat Japanese and Indian food, then I certainly would find no cause to interfere; eating while sitting on the floor can be fun. But no, these people eat on the floor for every meal not because they want to, but because baby likes to climb. She likes to climb up their chairs and onto the table.

Instead of teaching their baby not to climb the dining room chairs onto the table, they have taken away all the tools for teaching by removing the chairs. They have become slaves to their offspring, a tiny person not much bigger than a Thanksgiving turkey, who has been on this planet just a little over a year. I have hair older than this little girl, and yet she has two grown-ups in a tailspin, rearranging their house to suit her fifteen-month-old whims. This is a family whose house is a maze of gates and barriers (she's a climber!), where every danger is hidden or cushioned, to guard against accidents. Over the holidays, they put their Christmas tree in a cramped, back guest room instead of in the front room, because they were afraid the little one would pull it down.

Mommy told me she *tried* eating her lunch while sitting in a chair at the table. She tried, but her child kept climbing the chair in an attempt to get onto the table. After faintly intoning "No!" a few times, Mommy knelt on the floor, *at the table,* and continued eating her lunch. This worked for a few minutes, until her child decided it would be fun to stand on Mommy's calves. Mommy continued eating her burrito with thirty extra pounds standing on her calves. Ow! I imagine that if baby told Mommy to hold still for a painful head-stomping, Mommy would, with a sigh, oblige. Why, Mommy? Why?

"Get down, honey," you say in sweet, halfhearted mommy talk. "We don't climb on the chairs."

Oh yes, we do, your little demon thinks to herself, looking you straight in the eye.

"Honey, can you get down from the table now?" Your child, by this time, is surely laughing at you. Laughing, but incredulous, because you refuse to take a stand. *Look at me,* she is thinking. *I am crawling on your table! I am grabbing food off your plates! Doesn't that just frost you? I am making a mess, and all you can do is wheedle in that ridiculous voice, and ask me if I don't think it's time to get down.*

What a weenie your child must think you are, as she helps herself to the pepper shaker and flings it across the table.

Here's a tip: Pick her up and tell her that no, she is not allowed to climb the chairs at mealtime. No, she is not allowed to crawl on the table. No, she is not allowed to pull down the Christmas tree, throw cutlery, slap Mommy, or flush toys down the toilet. Pick her up and carry her someplace else, and talk to her firmly about why she may not do these things. Let her know that you are in charge, and that you all have to live together and work as a team. She will understand, even at fifteen months old.

Be consistent. Pick your child up and talk to her every time she behaves badly. If nothing else, she will agree to behave so that the incessant talking will stop. Bore her to tears with the talking. Deal with your child, and communicate honestly with her. Be a grown-up, because that is your job. Show your child that you are good at your job. Expect your children to act like kind, thoughtful individuals, even if they are toddlers and you think they are too young to understand. When you hand the authority over to your child, he is not learning the value of sharing, and worse, he is learning that you are helpless, wishy-washy, and indecisive. If you have a daughter, these are probably not the kind of attributes you would like her to have when she is a grown-up. If you have a son, you probably don't want him thinking he can walk all over the women in his life. But that is exactly the kind of behavior you are modeling to your children.

If you never set boundaries, your children will continue to push the edge of the envelope until you are old before your time and your friends don't want to visit you anymore. You are not doing your children any favors. Teach them how to get along in the world by presenting them with real-world examples. In the real world, they will not get to climb on chairs and tables. If they have an obvious gift in their chair-and-table climbing, then the circus or mountaineering could be an excellent choice for their future employment. Until that time, you won't be stifling their athletic or creative spirits by teaching them some manners. Don't tiptoe around your child anymore; she won't bite. And if she does, you've been letting her get away with this stuff for far too long.

Next Christmas, you might try lashing the tree to the wall, as a backup to firmly escorting your child into another room for a long talk on the rudeness—and danger—of pulling down the family Christmas tree. Now, go be in charge, because someone has to be. And you're the grown-up, remember?

CHAPTER 5

CHLOE, SWEETHEART, MOMMY HAS TO SPEAK IN THE THIRD PERSON NOW!

WHAT IS WITH THE BABY TALK AMONG GROWN WOMEN WITH children, and the speaking in the third person? Doesn't it sound kind of creepy? I'm sure you've heard those mothers of toddlers sitting with their friends at the park or at the coffeehouse:

> "Sweetie, come sit with Mommy now. Mommy wants you to come and have your snack. Can you bring the ball to Mommy?"

I guess I missed the memo that informed all of us mothers that our children wouldn't understand the words "me" and "I," and therefore the word "Mommy" must be used instead. Or perhaps such a woman is identifying herself to the world. In case the people in her vicinity are still in the dark about her status as a mother, they will now be reminded every time she opens her mouth to her child.

"Mommy said not to do that, honey. Mommy does not like that behavior. Come sit with Mommy. Mommy wants to talk to you."

Mommy is starting to sound as if she's rounding the bend, just a hair. Does Mommy think that if she says, "I told you not to hit Dylan with the dump truck! Come here RIGHT NOW!" it will bruise her child's precarious self-esteem? Perhaps Mommy thinks it will soften the blow of her reprimand if she refers to herself as another person entirely. *I didn't say that, Mommy did! And she said it in a very sweet voice!*

And then there is the inexplicable habit of making your child's name a diminutive, even if the name clearly begs to be left alone. The Tom-Toms, Bry-Brys, and Kevvies:

"Ry-Ry, that wasn't nice when you kicked the kitty. Can Ry-Ry bring the nice kitty to Mommy?"

Ry-Ry didn't get to hear this just when he was eighteen months or two years old; no, his name is Ryan, and even though he's eight years old his mommy and daddy still address him as "Ry-Ry" when they are being cuddly, or trying to call his attention to certain infractions, or trying to get him to pick up his room, or attempting to extricate his hands from the throat of another child. They sweetly intone "Ry-Ry" when he's in a belligerent mood and they want him to cooperate. He is in a belligerent mood quite a lot. It hasn't yet occurred to these parents that speaking to their child as if he is still a toddler might perhaps be contributing to the fact that their child still often acts like a toddler, albeit a bigger and meaner one.

I have a friend who, despite being intelligent, articulate, and the possessor of a highly developed sense of humor, still speaks baby talk to her children. It's more than a little disconcerting to be in the middle of a conversation with her and have her turn to address her children. Her voice rises about an octave, and a cheerful—some might say shrill—yet musical lilt creeps into her voice. It was bad enough when her kids were really young, but her children are now ten and twelve years old. And, strangely, they don't seem to hear a word she says. Could there be a connection? Her children, who are mostly sullen and unpleasant, look at her as if she is slightly insane. The trouble is, she does sound slightly insane, because she is talking to these junior bad boys as if they are all in the land of Buttercups and Candy Floss, and everything is Happy Happy Happy, and if I speak like Miss Nancy long enough, everything really will be all right, won't it, Mr. Green Jeans?

Please stop. It didn't work when your child was four, and it's really embarrassing now that you have teenagers. Raising your voice to a high pitch and lisping like a five-year-old does not inspire respect, nor does it give an overwhelming impression of authority. It gives the impression, in fact, that you are being held hostage and are trying to soothe your captors by not alarming them with an authoritative voice. Perhaps you are being held hostage by your children and do not want to anger them by sounding too firm or confident. But they can smell the fear, and the baby voice just makes you a target.

Practice speaking in the self-assured tones of a grown-up. Picture your children as responsible individuals, and address them accordingly. Perhaps when you start treating them like responsible individuals, they will start behaving as such.

You'll save your vocal cords, your friends won't think you're a whack job, and your children may come to appreciate your newfound respect for them.

Why put up one more barrier between you and your growing child? *You* probably wouldn't want to spend much time with someone who spoke to you as if you had the relative IQ of a schnauzer. Let's make the same assumption about your children. No matter what age they may be.

CHAPTER 6

TELEPHONE ETIQUETTE: IT'S FOR MOMS AND DADS, TOO!

YOU FEEL LIKE TALKING TO AN OLD FRIEND. YOU DON'T GET together as much as you used to before you both had kids—mostly because you find your friend has a slightly higher level of tolerance for chaos and noise and rampaging youngsters than you do—but you do speak on the phone once in a while, because sometimes you just really need to talk to an old friend. So you dial the number, your friend answers, and much hello-ing and happy greeting sounds ensue. You ask if she can talk, because, you tell her, it's been one of those days, and you're having a little meltdown. You hear the sound of kids in the background, and you suddenly realize that she's been conversing with her child.

Your friend's child began the incessant pestering the moment the phone was answered, and your friend could not bring herself to say "Not now, honey, I'm talking on the phone" with any kind of authority. This child may have been perfectly content finger-painting off in the corner, but the minute Mommy's attention was diverted by a phone call, there was suddenly a multitude of pressing concerns that had to be dealt with at that moment, and the little darling's burning need for attention could not wait until the end of a five-minute phone call.

There are few things more annoying than talking on the phone with a friend and realizing in the middle of a sentence that she is actually having a parallel conversation with her child. While you were baring your soul, her child asked a question, so she just went ahead and answered it, without so much as a "Sorry, could you hang on a minute?" This sort of thing makes me incredibly cranky, and I usually suggest that maybe we should talk at a more convenient time. Inexplicably, these people can never seem to understand why I would want to talk later, when we just got on the phone. Hmm.

And then it comes: the inevitable "Hey! Hang on, do you want to say hi to Logan?!" It's not actually a question, because already she's gone, having passed the phone to her three-year-old. "Actually," you say, hoping she'll hear you before the phone gets passed, "maybe I should call back. When would be a good time to . . ." But your words disappear into the ether, or else are heard only by the perplexed toddler on the other end of the line, who is breathing heavily into the receiver.

"Hi, Logan!" you say, with weary resignation and a half-hearted dollop of perk. "How ya doing?"

There is more heavy breathing. Heavy, wet breathing, and some tiny sound that might be "Hello," or simply Logan trying to figure out where the voice is coming from.

"Logan? Tell your mommy to get back on the phone." More heavy breathing. "Logan? Tell your mommy I am going to call back. Logan. Get Mommy." The heavy breathing stops, which probably means he has put the receiver down. Your friend picks it up, briefly, to inform you that "Emma wants to say hi!" The phone is handed to the baby. You are on the telephone with a fourteen-month-old child, who sounds as if she is trying to eat the receiver.

I know that you want your children to have practice speaking on the telephone, and sometimes we enjoy having little conversations with your children when we call. But you really have to stop that habit you have of just handing the phone over to infants and assorted toddlers, a habit almost as bad as letting your child interrupt every telephone conversation. When I call you on the telephone, you should assume that I am calling because I want to talk to you. At the end of the conversation, if you feel an urgent need for your children to speak on the telephone, you may ask me if I would like to speak to the little cherubs. The key word is "ask." "Asking" is different from "telling," and it invites the person you are "asking" to exercise their decision-making skills. You may "ask," and I will then be able to make a decision, based on my time and inclination, and whether I want to stay on the phone for an extra ten minutes and listen to some heavy breathing and/ or that adorable Martian voice saying, "Hi! Hi! Hi!" This is doubly true if I am calling long-distance.

They really do sound cute on the phone, and I enjoy calling my own house for that very reason, just to hear that adorable Martian voice saying, "Hi, Mama," in a way that makes it seem as if he is really pleased to be talking on the phone with me. But that's me calling my own child. A friend might not find the sound of my child's tiny voice quite as precious as I do. That's why it's always best to ask.

I've got friends with daughters who all instinctively understood, while still in diapers, what to do with a telephone. One girl we know was, by the age of two and a half, able to dial her grandma's number and talk while simultaneously twirling the telephone cord with her fingers, a talent I didn't think kicked in until a girl was about thirteen.

When my oldest boy was two, he was only dimly aware of what a telephone was, and certainly lacked the keen skills required to speed-dial and twirl the cord. By the age of five, he could talk into a telephone, but cautiously, holding it away from his ear and glancing suspiciously at it from time to time. He always seemed slightly startled by the unlikely sound of human voices coming out of the receiver, and looked as if he'd like to poke the receiver with a stick and then throw it up in the air. This lasted until he was about, oh, fourteen years old.

Both my boys were taught to answer the phone politely and identify themselves to callers, but my oldest never quite got the hang of it, and usually avoided answering it altogether. My youngest son took to the telephone as would an eager young social secretary, running to answer after the first ring, identifying himself immediately to all callers, and actually writing down names and messages. We had to work on his answering skills, however, as, in his zeal, he often gave callers more information than we might have preferred.

For instance, the question "May I please speak to your dad?" should not be met with "Daddy's on the toilet having a big poop. May I take a message?" An inquiry as to whether your mother is home is best not answered with "Mommy is taking a little nap," especially if it's around noon.

Teach your child that a simple "Hello, this is Jackson speaking" is a helpful way to answer the phone. For when Mom or Dad isn't available, explain how to ask someone for their name and number, and how to write down the collected information. If that is more than your child can manage, teach him to politely ask the caller to call back. And, of course, there is always modern technology, for those times when it's best just to let the "machine" answer the phone. But do teach your children to have nice phone voices, so that they don't end up like so many sullen teens, who answer the phone with barely perceptible grunts. Do not let your child grow into a teenage cliché. Teach your offspring to answer the telephone with a well-enunciated and clear voice, and a polite, helpful demeanor, so that the person on the other end won't have to awkwardly ask "What?" and "Excuse me?" too many times.

Several children of my acquaintance answer the telephone very nicely, but still seem mystified as to what is supposed to happen next. For instance, the daughter of a friend picks up the phone and says hello, to which I say, "Hi, how are you?" Good, she answers, so I ask, "Is your mom home?"

"Yeah!" she replies enthusiastically.

Then there is a long, long pause. She waits expectantly. I wait expectantly.

We have established that her mother is home, but she doesn't seem to realize that this is her cue to find her mom and tell her she has a phone call. More time elapses, until I finally say, "So! Well! Perhaps I could, ah, speak to her?"

"Sure!" she says cheerfully, and off she goes. This is endlessly entertaining, and I always wonder when the light bulb is going to go on.

Cheerfulness and enthusiasm are always appreciated, but also clue your children in to basic phone-answering protocol, to save them from embarrassment and to give them invaluable tools for their future telephoning careers. A quick tutorial might come in handy, just to give your child a sample of responses. Not only will their skills on the telephone be a big help to you, but the sound of competent children really is just adorable. It might make us more apt to want to have a conversation with them.

CHAPTER 7

THE PRINCESS AND THE
FREE-RANGE ORGANIC PEA

WE KNOW A COUPLE WHO HAVE A DARLING LITTLE GIRL.
Unfortunately, we don't see much of them since they became
parents. Their little hothouse flower must be home by five
o'clock so she can be fed in her own special chair, bathed in
her own bathtub with her familiar squeezy whale, wrapped in
her own cuddly blankie while her favorite book is read to her,
and then tucked into her bed by seven o'clock, every single
night, come hell or high water. And it's not just her night-
times that are so highly regulated. She is whisked home from
morning playdates and carried off from afternoon parties,
should these activities encroach on her morning or afternoon
naptimes. She is ferried home in broad daylight, *put in her paja-
mas,* and tucked into her crib. After the drawing of the curtains, a sign is placed on the front door that reads, "Shh! Baby
Sleeping!" Precious? Adorable. It doesn't at all make you want
to start banging garbage-can lids on the front porch.

Yes, getting your children used to a reasonably early bedtime is important, and consistency is a standard for which we

all should strive. But there is a point at which you must step back from your regimented life and ask yourselves some questions. No, really, have a seat, because there are a lot of questions:

Have you, perhaps, placed so much importance on your child's schedule that you have neglected your family's social life? Do your friends, who can barely remember what you look like, continue to meet for dinners and parties with one another, with and without their children? Do you avoid popping over to a friend's house for a spontaneous get-together because your children have never slept in a Portacrib and it might scare them? Have you stopped going out in the evening altogether because you don't want to disrupt your child's "routine"? Has the parade passed you by?

And what about those times when a warm bath and a story, not to mention your child's own bed and blanket, are unavailable? Has your child been programmed to live such a rarefied existence that you can't put her down in someone else's spare room for a nap? Will you have to postpone that trek across Australia or that trip to Hawaii for the next ten years because your child cannot deviate from his routine, even for the sake of a vacation?

You should be running the vacuum cleaner, turning the volume up on the radio, and having a dance party when your infants are napping, so that they won't startle awake when they hear a dog barking in the next county. Just as it's good for them to become accustomed to the daily noise of life during their naptimes, it's also beneficial for them to get used to being in strange places and unfamiliar surroundings. Have your child try falling asleep, every now and then, in a room other than her own. A friend's spare room, with the large Godzilla poster looking down from the wall and that kit-kat clock with the disconcertingly moving eyes, may not have that comforting *Goodnight Moon* décor; there may be a dearth of stuffed animals crowded on the shelves. But there's a bed, and if your child is tired, wouldn't it be nice if she could go down for a little sleep, so you could continue visiting with the grown-ups in the other room? And she will, if she's had a little practice.

If she misses one nap, she might be a little cranky later, but it won't be the end of the world. If you get your children used to adapting to all kinds of bedtime situations, it will only make things easier as they grow older, when they are invited on their first sleepover, or if you decide you want to celebrate your spouse's birthday into the wee hours. And if your child is able to sleep through marching bands, earthquakes, and the sound of Daddy and his friends playing vintage Flying Burrito Brothers at two in the morning, entertaining at home becomes a whole lot easier.

When our first child was a baby, we tried to establish a regular routine, and I will, under pressure, admit to scheduling many of our evenings around his bedtime. It is true that when you finally do manage to get your children to fall asleep by themselves at a reasonable hour, you hate to rock the boat. But we relaxed our expectations before too long, and because of a family illness we were on the road with him when he was just a few days old. He had no choice but to adapt to unfamiliar lodgings. We had a nice bedtime ritual every night; it just wasn't always in the same bath, in the same bed, with the same nightlight. Our child did become accustomed to falling asleep in strange beds, and grew up to be fairly adaptable.

Perhaps you remember the story of the Princess and the Pea: the Princess was so sensitive that she felt a tiny pea that had been placed under a hundred mattresses. If you are hoping to marry your little girl off to a prince with a neurotic mother, then you are doing a fine job, but as far as getting her used to real life, you might as well be raising her in a plastic bubble.

And what's with the bath every night, with the hair-washing and the bubbles and the antibacterial soap? Your child doesn't need a full delousing every day; she's a child—children are supposed to be a little grubby. Give her hair and skin a break. Wipe her down with a wet washcloth if she's been using her face as a canvas for blueberry yogurt, teach her to keep her hands clean, and hose her down in the bathtub if she's taken to rolling in the dirt a bit too vigorously. A nice warm bath is a lovely idea before bed, but there's no need to call in the Hazmat team for a full sterilization.

Yes, when you are in your own house, you want to exert as much control as possible, setting a standard of no sweets, strictly organic produce, and a regimented bedtime ritual. But it might do you and your child some good to learn how to be a little more flexible. Encouraging adaptability not only gives you more freedom to get out into the world, but will prepare your child for the many curveballs that life is apt to throw.

CHAPTER 8

CHILDREN'S FURNITURE: WHY?

DO YOU REALLY NEED THAT ADORABLE THREE-THOUSAND-dollar Adirondack bedroom set sized for a three-year-old? A small bed shaped like a race car and a set of Lilliputian patio furniture may look really cool in the showroom, but think this through; someone in the marketing department (who clearly has no children of his own) has figured out a way to sell you all a precious and adorably tiny bill of goods.

I imagine some fresh-faced go-getter at a large conference table saying, "They loved the reproduction Eames bent-plywood dining room chairs, so why not make a really small version for the kids?"

"But sir," ventures some second-level design lackey who clearly has no vision, "won't the kids grow out of those little chairs just a few years after the chairs are purchased?"

The entire conference table laughs heartily, and an industry is born.

Those of you who pined for a dollhouse as a child may now purchase, for very grown-up prices, miniature versions of fabulous bedroom suites, living room furniture, and outdoor dining sets for your youngsters. As Dorothy Parker once famously said, it's enough, dear reader, to make you "fwow up."

When I was a child, I longed for a giant four-poster bed hung with curtains, and other stylish décor involving velvet and brocade. I even bought myself a brass door knocker with my allowance (Why?), which my mother graciously allowed me to put on my bedroom door. I actually asked for a chandelier for my birthday. My mother knew of my extravagant tastes and sympathized but, being a sensible person, didn't feel the need to rush out and fulfill my burning eleven-year-old desires. She was also aware that I wanted to trek to Morocco, be a spy, and travel on the Orient Express, but, well, fat chance. Whether or not she was afraid of the potential for long-term damage to my fragile psyche we will never know, but she somehow managed to restrain herself from indulging my every youthful whim. Had she indulged my every whim, we would have been flying off in hot-air balloons and the house would have looked like one of William Randolph Hearst's hangovers.

And yet we now have entire industries devoted to helping parents fulfill either their children's dreams or the dreams they assume their children have. The prepackaged, predecorated life is now available for the under-five set, complete with wall hangings and other accessories that used to be of the more handmade variety.

Children are having their bedroom suites made over as often as their wardrobes, and from the elaborately decorated nurseries to the richly decked-out playrooms complete with "wall systems," two-hundred-dollar tepees, and craft tables, things have gotten completely out of hand. "Over the top" does not even come close to describing the ornate décor made exclusively for children. And when your child grows out of that cherry-veneer sleigh bed in a matter of months, you will be stuck with a roomful of expensive, doll-sized furniture.

You are being sold a "media space" for little Ashton, suitable to hold the giant flat-screen TV you will be putting in his room. And don't forget the miniature "director's chair" for your little Madison, because she's a star! In case she doesn't feel quite special enough, you can have her name monogrammed on the back.

You can purchase colorful "gallery frames," in which you may put your children's precious artwork, or perhaps those nautically themed pictures you've bought to go with the boat-shaped bunk beds and "Chesapeake Bay" workstation. You are not buying your child a bed or a desk; you are purchasing a lifestyle, one that you hope will say, "Look! I have Old Money! We summer at Martha's Vineyard!"

These child-centered catalogs, which you will receive at a dizzying rate if you ever purchase so much as a sock from one, are full of little blond, blue-eyed moppets who frolic happily in their gigantic playrooms, which have been deco-rated to within an inch of their lives. "Summer" playrooms, train-themed playrooms, classic-sports playrooms. The "Retro Kitchen" playroom has more shiny appliances than my real-life house. Who wouldn't want a bright pink front-loading washer and dryer and matching streamlined fridge and sink? But do you really need to buy it for your five-year-old for nine hundred dollars?

A certain trendy grown-up furniture store, in addi-tion to hawking fashionable pint-sized furnishings, now has a "Teen" catalog. To go with one of your ultracool teenage bedroom suites, you can purchase clean, shiny, painted metal "lockers," in which your teen can store his clothing and sun-dries. Presumably so he can feel like a real-life grungy teen who attends a real-life public school and hangs out at the lockers, but without the drab gray colors and graffiti, or the bother of actually having to attend the local public school.

For a hefty price, your child can appear to be a hip street version of himself. Beds with modish surfboard-shaped headboards, matching surfboard tables, and retro island wall hangings will surely make him feel like he's a real surfer, even though he may not regularly hang ten at the local pipes. He may, in fact, spend most of his free time glued to the screen of his computer playing video games, but whoa, that shag rug ($200) and the rusty metal "Beach Cabana" sign ($75) that hangs over his distressed wood beach-house desk ($550) will certainly make him feel like the itinerant beach bum with whom you think he identifies. Or is it you who longed to be a beach bum when you were fifteen? Come on, really, did you? Because imagine: If you really had, at the age of fourteen or fifteen, wanted to present yourself to the world as a carefree surfin' dude, how might you have reacted if you came home from school one day to find that your parents had outfitted your room in a complete "Rusty's Surf Shack" motif? Wouldn't you have been, like, totally embarrassed?

I must at least let you know that my mother did, in fact, indulge me the year I inexplicably begged for my own chandelier. She took me to the light-fixture store and let me pick out a forty-dollar chandelier, which seemed highly extravagant at the time. It was my only birthday present, and one of my favorite gifts ever.

Of course life is too short not to go floating off in hot-air balloons. And of course you should decorate your house like Barbara Eden's Arabian Nights fantasy genie bottle, if that's what you really want to do. It's your house. But do it for *you,* not because you're being emotionally blackmailed by a ten-year-old. Presumably, the furniture you'll be buying for yourself won't be too small for you in six months.

CHEAP DECORATING TIPS!

🍸 🍸 🍸

WHY THROW ALL THAT MONEY AWAY WHEN YOU CAN DECO-rate your child's room like a real surf bum's crash pad for mere pennies?! Paint is a relatively inexpensive decorating option, and a couple of coats of a tropical hue for the walls is a good start, along with a mattress on the floor. In fact, put that mattress on the floor as soon as your little one is out of the crib, as we did. He won't have as far to fall, should he roll out of bed in the middle of the night during an earthquake, and as he grows older, it will provide a great place to lounge with books and friends. And there's no room for dust bunnies to collect underneath! Instead of that faux-distressed desk and bookshelf, shop at your local thrift store or Goodwill, saving hundreds of dollars while recycling unat-tractive furniture, which will somehow look really hip painted with fuchsia-colored enamel. Skip the overpriced media center; your child does not need a television in his bedroom. Really. A few plastic fish nailed to the wall will complete the look.

Figure that by the time your child graduates from high school, college tuition will be up around $100,000 a year. The cost of several mini bedroom, playroom, and patio suites, wisely invested, might buy little Lola a year at Vassar, not including books and food, so start extolling the utter hipness of molded plastic chairs from the ninety-nine-cents store, and start saving now!

CHAPTER 9

ADVENTURES IN BABYSITTING

IF YOUR CHILD HAS BEEN GIVEN LOTS OF CARE, NURTURING, and attention, she will eventually feel secure enough with Mommy and Daddy's love to easily feel comfortable with a new caregiver. This is to be hoped for. This is a good thing. This will enable you to get *out of the house,* use your arms/swear freely for a few hours, and, possibly, eat a hot meal with both hands.

This maneuver is often easier to describe than to actually perform. For instance, when our first child was a baby, it took us a while to figure out that the dramatic, despondent cries we heard as we guiltily left the house stopped not long after the babysitter distracted him with something shiny.

We had earlier attempted a number of different ways of extricating ourselves from our house, a few of which you may have already tried at home.

Plan A: The Thoughtful Explanation
Baby's conscientious daddy spends a nice hour explaining exactly where we will be going and what we are going to be doing (except for the drinking and dancing-on-tables part),

telling the child what kind of games he will be playing with his babysitter, how much fun he will have, and how Mommy will kiss him when we come home. A one-sided discussion such as this may take a little time, but it will make you feel all warm and devoted, and alleviate the guilt of leaving your child. Just be sure Mommy gets in on the chat before the sitter arrives, because once Daddy has finished with the long explanation, you don't want to have to spend the same amount of time explaining that, yes, he meant Mommy was going, too.

When the sitter arrives and you wave bye-bye, the screaming generally starts up anyway.

Plan B: The Long Good-bye

The babysitter arrives. You sit with your child just a tiny bit longer, incorporating the babysitter into whatever game you are playing. As you start to rise from your spot on the floor, your child demands "just one more" game of checkers, "one more" game of Chutes and Ladders, or, the clincher, "one more cuddle." You explain that his friend Kelly is here, and that he will have so much fun with his friend, and that Mommy and Daddy are going out for just a tiny little while and will be back really soon and will give him all the cuddles in the world. You spend another half hour playing "Go Fish," and another half hour after that reading a story to your child, because he took exception when you put on your coat to leave. After another twenty minutes of puzzles, you calculate how much you will be paying your babysitter at the end of the evening. When you finally tear yourself away after saying what you hope is a final good-bye, your child erupts into tears anyway.

Plan C: Exit Out the Back Door Without Your Child Seeing You
At one point we decided it would be less disruptive to leave the house without saying good-bye at all. This is not to say that we just slipped out, abandoning our despondent baby. Well, yes, we did. But earlier in the day we explained that we would be going out to dinner. When the time came to leave, we didn't make a big production out of it, and we congratulated ourselves heartily for managing a clean getaway while our son was playing happily with his babysitter. It wasn't until we were in the car that we realized we had left the address of our intended destination inside the house. Sheepishly tiptoeing in through the back door, avoiding the babysitter's incredulous, horror-stricken face as she realized that her nice, quiet evening was about to end, we grabbed the address and tore out of the driveway as the faint strains of "Crying Child in D Major" wafted through the night air. Do not make this mistake.

Perhaps you have noticed that each plan ended with the same response. A crying child is not a fait accompli, but if your child has not yet reached the age of reason, you must know that he will do everything in his power to keep you with him. It is part of his age, and his nature, and his instinct; just as a joey burrows in his mother's pouch or a recently beheaded chicken runs around in circles, like Pavlov's puppy, your child sees you heading out the door, and the waterworks begin.

Yes, it might seem difficult, at first, attempting to leave the house after your two-year-old has clamped on to your left ankle, showing no indication of loosening his grip. Drag him along as best you can (he should enjoy the exciting slide along the floor!), but at the door, hand him firmly over to the baby-sitter, planting a good kiss on his tearstained cheek. You must trust that, moments after you leave, before you even reach the car door, his tears will have miraculously dried, and he will be happily playing with this new, presumably attentive, often younger- and prettier-than-you stranger.

It's not as if you go gallivanting around town all that often. You know you need an evening out, and although it is tempting to never go out again because the angst of leaving is almost too much to bear, do not let the "just one more" power play deter you. The pain of separation is probably harder on you than on your child. Your children really won't suffer permanent psychological damage from being left with a babysitter for a few hours, especially if you can procure a reasonably caring caregiver. Do your best to find a reliable and trustworthy person, preferably someone who at least likes your children.

Should you feel some trepidation about leaving your child in the hands of an unknown teenager for that first big night out, do a few trial runs beforehand. Leave for an hour or two at a time, until you all feel more comfortable.

If you answer the door with your toddler in tow and the new babysitter immediately locates the TV and refrigerator before making eye contact with your child, this could indicate that your child will be of secondary importance to the potential caregiver. Perhaps, if your child is a talker, you'll find out if the babysitter talked to him at all, or if she spent the entire time glued to reality TV.

If you are the kind of person who micromanages your child's life, you may need to let go of the idea that you are in total control when you leave your child with a babysitter. You shouldn't expect a teenage babysitter to wash the dishes, vacuum, and dust in addition to playing games, feeding your child dinner, bathing him, getting him to brush his teeth, and tucking him in after a nice bedtime story. You will be lucky if the sitter is able to feed him reheated pizza before putting him to bed with his clothes on. If a game of checkers can be squeezed in, count yourself lucky. It's perfectly fair to lay down some rules for sitters; after all, *you* are paying *them*. For instance, I prefer that my kids don't watch *Coeds Gone Wild* or, in fact, any regular TV programming, so I circumvent this problem by letting them pick out a movie ahead of time. I tell

the sitter to please watch her own TV shows after the kids are asleep, but if the kids want to watch anything, they've already picked their own movie.

For a short while, we had one of those babysitters who seemed too good to be true. She would cheerfully arrive with a backpack full of games to play, and we would come home to find her pitching baseballs to the kids. The dishes would be cleaned, the kitchen spotless. She was fifteen years old, and, of course, that kind of overachiever does not last long in the babysitting game. She got too busy with her violin playing and marathon running, advanced-placement classes and finding a solution for Middle East peace. We had to look elsewhere.

We have some friends whose babysitter loves their kids, and their children adore spending the evening with this babysitter, obviously because she is young, cheerful, and fun. Also, she lets them jump on the furniture and stay up late eating sweets. Our friends know that if they get home before eleven at night there is a good chance that their children will still be up, jumping on the sofa and mainlining candy corn, but it's worth it to them, because they know their kids are safe and happy. The kids will also be extra tired the next day, and everyone may get to sleep in. "As long as no one's bleeding" is pretty much where these carefree parents draw the line.

Now, I might draw the line at the staying up until all hours and the cramming fists full of sweets into tiny mouths;

you might draw the line at something else. The point is, don't draw so many lines that you're out of a good babysitter. I'd take somebody who likes to read aloud and play games with the kids over someone who does all the dishes and polishes the stove. If you do find one of those dish-washing, baseball-pitching, story-reading, dinner-cooking, babysitting freaks of nature, consider putting this paragon on retainer, or at least setting up a guaranteed regular babysitting night. This babysitter will probably be heading off to an Ivy League university on a full scholarship within a matter of months, so make the most of this person while you still have the chance.

In the meantime, you can hope for a babysitter who is fairly responsible, well-mannered, and good-hearted; sometimes that is all you need.

YOUR TEEN:
A PRECIOUS UNTAPPED RESOURCE

IF YOU HAVE TWO OR MORE CHILDREN, START TALKING *to the oldest at an early age about how he will "get to babysit" when he gets to be twelve years old. Build on the idea that great power will be his, and that along with great power comes great responsibility. Float the possibility that he may even be remunerated for his time and labor, and by the time he is nearing his twelfth birthday, he will be begging to babysit his younger sibling.*

My oldest son, half a year before his twelfth birthday, came up with what he thought was a great way to celebrate his special day. He suggested that instead of having a birthday party, his dad and I should go out to dinner and let him babysit. An awfully thoughtful idea, but we gave him a little party instead. Soon after that, he became our very handy, very available, very favorite babysitter. And cheap? Yes, the price is right, of course, as we have arranged a special Family Discount. He rarely does the dishes, but I know he'll get his brother to bed at a pretty reasonable hour, and he's got the fairly responsible, good-hearted thing going for him. Best of all, we don't need to drive him home!

CHAPTER 10

YOUR TWELVE-YEAR-OLD GYM RAT

LITTLE BRIANNA HAS STARTED DISCUSSING THE FAT CONTENT of her meals, and wailing about the amount of *carbs* she ate the night before. She knows that Mommy goes to the gym, and she, too, longs to wear a mint-green terry velour sweatsuit and walk on a treadmill while discussing diets and hair products. So what to do when your twelve-year-old tries to convince you that she needs her own gym membership? No, she'd rather not go with her mom and exercise—what, are you wack? She wants her own membership.

If your children are in need of, well, serious physical exercise, I would say that you or your spouse should enlist them in regular activities, whether at the gym or at the park. But if my very young daughter begged me for an expensive gym membership, I might mention that there is another alternative to joining a gym. It may be a radical suggestion, but I would suggest to my child that she go out and *play*.

Playing could be a concept with which your daughter is unfamiliar, especially if she has been wearing three-inch-high platform shoes, midriff tops, and low-rise skirts since the age of four, any of which make it nearly impossible to engage in cart-wheels, leaping, handball, or racing. She may have forgotten that brief childhood moment when she played hopscotch and Chinese jump rope in the schoolyard, so, much as if administering regressive therapy, you might need to reintroduce her to the idea of playing. Set aside a little time each day, after school. Give her a jump rope, along with the directive to master Red Hots, Cross Overs, and Skipping. Invite a friend over for her to play with. Suggest that instead of pulling their chairs up to the computer to troll for cute boys on MySpace, they run around and get some fresh air. Your preteen may balk at first, but the fact is, she doesn't get to have her own gym member-ship yet. Why? Because you said so. That is why. *You said so.* Practice these four lovely little words: "Because I said so!" See how easy and satisfying they are to say?

Sign her up for soccer, or basketball, or softball. She doesn't have to be the next Mia Hamm, but she'll certainly get to run around a little in the outdoors, and possibly learn to enjoy a hobby other than shopping. Tell her that the brain-power required to count fat grams and tally up carbohydrate calories could otherwise be used learning to speak Italian or reading to the elderly. Suggest that she consider doing both, as a way to exercise those parts of her brain inexplicably con-sumed by an intimate awareness of the body weights and BMIs of various female celebrities.

A HEALTH TIP: CUDDLING, SLEEP, AND YOUR ADOLESCENT

Y Y Y

IF YOU HAVE STOPPED CUDDLING YOUR ELEVEN- OR *twelve-year-old boy or girl because you think they have "outgrown it," immediately recommence. Now is the time to get your cuddles in. They are not yet too cool, and they are in a slightly befuddled state as to what "cool" is anyway. They do not realize how much they need the cuddling, but they do need it, and you do too. You do not have to cuddle them in front of friends, if they would find that embarrassing, but find time each day for some enforced cuddle sessions. Cuddling gives both parent and offspring a necessary feeling of well-being and helps cement a relationship that might otherwise start fraying around the edges with the onset of adolescence.*

As your children inch toward their teenage years, you will notice a few changes in their skin, mood, and attitude. To help alleviate possible problems, let your adolescents sleep as much as possible. In fact, if they can sleep through their entire adolescence, all the better for them. They will awake refreshed and invigorated,

➔

all grown-up and able to deal with the rigors of adulthood, with none of the debilitating self-esteem issues that often spring forth from those acne-laden and awkward teenage years. We all need more sleep, and teenagers need more than the average infant. And, like infants, if they don't get that much-needed sleep, they will be irritable, cranky, and more prone to tantrums.

CHAPTER II

IN CONSIDERATION OF OUR CHILDLESS FRIENDS

WOULD YOU THINK IT POLITE IF A SMOKER LIT UP A CIGAR, blew the smoke in your face, and then demanded that you admire the way the rings floated to the ceiling? Might you take issue with someone setting their boom box next to your spot on the park bench, cranking the volume, and then giving you a nasty look when you didn't get up and dance?

And yet this is what it must feel like to the individual who has chosen *not* to bring a bundle or two of unbridled joy into this world. People without children go about their business, usually bothering no one, and suddenly parents appear, using their designer strollers like battering rams and scattering pedestrians as they maneuver down the sidewalk. They spread out their abundant paraphernalia on every spare surface, taking up the entire aisle in the grocery store so that their darling angels can maneuver their own adorable miniature shopping carts, and whoever doesn't coo at the precious sight is a wet blanket. True, few people are likely to die of cancer or suffer permanent hearing loss from exposure to your screaming tot, but a formal scientific study hasn't yet been funded, and I wouldn't make any premature assumptions.

Even fellow parents, out for an evening unencumbered by their own miniature action accessories, might object to someone else's boisterous child being forced upon them. The point is, the public at large should not have to put up with your noisy, inconsiderate child.

This is not to say that my own children have never behaved badly, and it's not to say that I've never been an exasperated, inept mother. I have been known to say, "Oh *fine*, what*ever*," when pestered by a certain eight-year-old—who looks eerily like my mother—but generally speaking, my children are fairly polite, not prone to whining, and understand the value of a stern look. However, they are still children, and while children have the capacity to be adorable, charming, impish, and delightful, they have just as much capacity to be annoying. So I take certain steps to ensure that my own children don't go out into the world and annoy other people to an inordinate degree.

I think children need to earn people's admiration, just as any adult would. Simply having cherub cheeks and a coy manner does not win one my undying respect and devotion, especially if the cherub in question has just pawed the hors d'oeuvres and is running around my cocktail party squealing at a high decibel level.

I don't go around assuming people will like *me* just because I have a cute ponytail and can twirl my skirt. If it were that easy, the world wouldn't need Prozac and self-help books. So I go through life generally assuming, however erroneous this assumption may be, that most people don't adore children, and I have attempted to train my children to behave accordingly. If your children behaved more nicely, perhaps your single and/or childless friends would come around the house more often, for visits. If your children learned to be delightful companions, your single and/or childless friends might want to take them out to the bookstore, or for an ice-cream cone. Children often benefit from the acquaintance of an adult who isn't either related or a paid babysitter, and these bonds can last a lifetime.

If your child is not noisy and inconsiderate, then please disregard everything I've said. Come, meet me for a cup of coffee, and we'll sit and chat while our youngsters sit quietly with their needlepoint and adventure books. And when a complete stranger comes up to you to remark how delighted she is to see a couple of children sitting quietly and behaving like young ladies and gentlemen in a restaurant/on a train/in a coffeehouse, your satisfaction will be palpable.

A Helpful Hint!

HOW TO RECOGNIZE WHEN YOU'RE A PARENT IN TROUBLE

Y Y Y

1. *You're jotting down notes for the Christmas newsletter in April.*
2. *You decline invitations for parties because you're busy "scrapbooking."*
3. *You think "scrapbooking" is fun.*
4. *You still speak to your child in baby talk, even though he is ten years old.*
5. *You randomly change the rules in the middle of playing a game with your child, so as not to disturb his tenuous hold on the reality of winning and losing.*
6. *You let your child randomly change the rules of a game when he sees that he is losing.*
7. *You find yourself writing "Chloe's Mom" where it says "Name" on forms and applications.*

8. *You find yourself humming the themes of children's TV shows at odd times of the day, even when your children aren't around.*

9. *You're worried that your younger child will be mad at you because you bought her older sibling a bigger TV.*

10. *You sleep on the floor next to your child's bed when she has the sniffles.*

CHAPTER 12

PACKING UP TROUBLES
IN THE OLD KIT BAG

SO YOU'RE TAKING A TRIP WITH THE KIDS. DID I MENTION
that you should pack light? What I mean by that is, you should
pack really, really light. Really. *Light.* I am not kidding about
this. You will thank me later.

Many mommies and daddies on their way to, say, the
Speedy Mart around the corner might as well be embarking on
a month-long survival quest, considering how much stuff they
tend to pack in various backpacks and diaper bags. When planning a getaway, they think the amount of luggage they need
on any given trip must necessarily grow exponentially with
the length of the vacation. This kind of thinking only leads to
copious sweating in airport baggage claims, more sweating on
cobblestoned streets, and lots and lots of sweating, cursing,
and soft whimpering while walking up the three flights of nar-
row, winding stairs at that charming fisherman's cottage you
rented on the Cornish coast.

Whether you're away for six weeks or just a long weekend, you really don't need more than a couple of overnight

bags for a family of four. I'd like to say it just one more time: Pack light. Say it with me! Lay out whatever you think you need, then put half of it back. Then put back half of what's left. Think comfortable, think solid colors, think washable. Think "washable in a small sink."

If you have two youngsters, you can pack their things together in one carry-on. Or, better yet, pack your stuff with one child's, and your spouse's stuff with the other. One child can carry a bag with the extra toiletries; the other can carry a few books and indispensable toys to keep them both busy en route. The best option is to have each traveler carry their own backpack, packed with everything for the trip. If tiny third-world tots can haul water a mile to their hut every day, certainly your toddler can carry a small backpack.

Rather than packing five separate outfits for a week away, pack a few comfy black outfits. Part of the fun of a holiday is the freedom to maintain a dashing layer of grime, so that you feel like a rugged world traveler. A good red lipstick for Mom will pull together any travel-weary ensemble, and smart, packable hats and shawls distract the discerning eye from the worn and torn.

Last summer we were away from home for longer than we had ever been away. At the end of August we found ourselves leaving a hot, muggy city where our clothes stuck to our skin and arriving in a small town on the North Sea, where it felt like a storm was blowing in from Norway. A storm was, in fact, blowing in from Norway; hence the freezing cold, wet, gale-force winds. My seven-year-old had only a couple of thin T-shirts to wear, having left various sweaters and articles of clothing scattered across the last continent we'd visited. Luckily for us, a local church was having a jumble sale under an awning, and we soon found a small and serviceable quilted nylon parka with fake fur trim on the hood, with which my son was immediately smitten. It cost roughly ninety cents and was a lifesaver for the entire week. On the way home, we left it with a friend who had a young daughter, so we wouldn't have to take it all the way back to California.

Bring clothes you'll feel comfortable wearing, and small accessories to spice up your appearance when you get tired of looking at the same black T-shirt for three weeks. Bring books for reading in airports and train stations, and then give them to friends you meet on your travels, or trade them in for books you can read on your return trip. And whatever you do, don't pack the "wrong" toothpaste— the one your five-year-old won't brush with for the whole month.

CHAPTER 13

THE THREE-MARTINI LAYOVER

SINCE YOU'VE TAKEN YOUR SHOES OFF ONCE FOR THE NICE security man, why not take them off again while you're waiting for your delayed flight, and curl up with some books and magazines in that tiny area of vacant floor space at the gate? Spread out your stuff, using your luggage as backrests; pull out the small magnetic chess game you so wisely packed, along with that deck of cards.

This does not mean you should spread your kith and kin into the areas occupied by other travelers, nor should you give your children free rein to run about unchecked in the airport lounge. Be acutely aware that many people do not travel with children and might be enjoying a quiet read before they embark, or an hour or two free from high-pitched squealing.

Buy some postcards from one of the many conveniently located airport shops. Once you arrive at your destination, you may not have time to write Auntie Netta and Grandpa Mike, so why not have the kids start on a stack right there in the airport lounge? You can mail them before the plane takes off, thereby avoiding expensive international postage, and your friends and family are thus guaranteed at least one postcard from your trip. You may think the kids won't have much to say, having not yet left on their vacation, but to a child, the airport itself should provide plenty of material for interesting observations, and the recipients will surely feel flattered that postcards arrived so soon after your departure.

If you have children in the prewriting set: Write the recipient's address in a BIG BOX, and tell your toddler to draw a pretty picture AROUND THE BIG BOX. This will not only allow the mail carrier to read the address, but will give you enough time to read most of the newspaper while you sip a nice cappuccino.

A two- or three-hour layover between flights needn't be viewed as a long sentence in purgatory, and there are many ways to make the time pass more pleasantly.

For instance, we once had a stopover of about three hours in Miami, Florida, while returning from a vacation with another couple and their two children.

Eight days on a tropical beach was deemed not quite enough fun for their youngsters, so this couple decided that since we had three whole hours to kill, they and their two kids would spend it at a children's aquarium. Wouldn't that be fun?

Horrified at the idea of rushing off somewhere in order to further enrich the children, I suggested that we all meet back at the airport before our next flight. My husband, child, and I quickly hightailed it out to where a tall, handsome fellow in a smart uniform was hailing cabs. There's only one thing a person can possibly do with three hours in Miami. I asked the nice man to direct us to his favorite Cuban restaurant, and off we went.

We arrived back at the airport sated, happy, and reeking of garlic. Our friends arrived having spent the past three hours on a compulsory march through the aquarium with droves of raucous children, including their own. They were exhausted, and the children were exhausted. We thought we'd cheer them up with descriptions of our fragrant garlic soup and hot sandwiches full of ham and pickles, while they grimly ate their fast-food lunches.

Any rational adult would have thought, "Miami? Cuban food!" The kids might have thought the same, had they ever been exposed to anything other than pizza and hot dogs. But the parents were doing the deciding, and they decided to do what they thought the kids would want to do, or what would be best for the kids. The kids, frankly, were completely beat after eight days on a beach and were in no condition to do any deciding. I'm sure they figured the aquarium would be a swell idea, and why not? Mom and Dad were once again catering solely to them, planning a day they thought would make the kids happy.

Your children might benefit from a little less enrichment and a little more spontaneity, and you, from thinking a little less about how you can do even more for them.

Traveling, with or without children, is often rife with adversity, and layovers. Coming up with creative solutions for potentially adverse situations can be very rewarding, and can often be quite enjoyable—and delicious.

CHAPTER 14

THE SELF-SUFFICIENT CARRY-ON: YOUR CHILD

TAKING A TRIP WITH KIDS DOESN'T HAVE TO BE A CHORE, nor is it necessary to outfit them with a dizzying array of boredom-alleviating electronics, in the event that there might be, heaven forbid, some quiet time. A bucketful of Game Boys, Walkmans, and iPods; a set of earphones for each child; a portable DVD screen; and a suitcase crammed with movies are just more stuff to carry and will only serve to put a barrier between you and your possibly new surroundings. A healthy dose of tedium is good for children; it often gets their little minds thinking and questioning, which might benefit all of you in the long run.

Once, in an airport lounge waiting for a flight, we had the misfortune to be sitting near a daddy and a mommy carrying their boy, who appeared to be about four years of age. Mommy looked utterly done in, and we soon saw why.

The refrain of "Mommy! Mommy! Mommy! Mommy! Mommy! Mommy!" came at two- or three-minute intervals. "Mommy!" he would intone, in a particularly heinous whine.

"Mommy! Mommy Mommy Mommy! Mommy!" until Mommy would finally say, in her most faux-patient voice, "What is it, honey?" The insistent little demon would then exclaim loudly, "Mommy, look! Mommy! Mommy! I HAVE FIVE FINGERS!" or something equally momentous. The fingers were then suitably cooed over, the boy's intelligence and insight were soundly commended, and three minutes later, it would start again. "MOMMY! Mommy! Mommy! Mommy! Mommy Mommy Mommy Mommy!! LOOK, Mommy. Mommy. Mommy." Until we were all ready to scream, "WHAT? WHAT IS IT? IN THE NAME OF ALL THAT IS HOLY, WHAT DO YOU WANT?" We could see the dark circles visibly forming under this woman's eyes. Somebody was going to get hurt, and at that moment I was grateful for the strict rules governing weaponry in airports.

Daddy, looking insouciant in his sweats and backward baseball cap, pretty much ignored the relentless refrain, occasionally chiming in "Wow!" or "Hey, Champ, that's great!" But they were clearly not impressed with their child's five fingers, and it must have been obvious to him, because he kept hammering away, trying to interest them in his thumb, or the news that he could make a fist.

While a long wait in an airport is a wonderful opportunity to relax with a good book, what do you do if your children have no interest in books? What if they are interested in nothing but their mommy's and daddy's full, undivided attention for every single minute? It will be the longest wait of your life.

Did this child not get enough Mommy and Daddy time at home, or did Mommy spend all her time with him, thereby rendering him incapable of entertaining himself or knowing how to enjoy time alone? If you introduce your child to the world of books at an early age, it will pay untold dividends in later years, when you need to kill time in cars, waiting rooms, and airports. Then, when you are in the airport waiting for that plane, it will be a colossal treat when you let the children pick out their own books to read. If it's an especially long flight, a puzzle book might be a good addition. Show your child how to use maze and puzzle books at home, and get him a stack for those times when he needs something to do. Something to do that does not involve Mommy. (Mommy! Mommy!) Familiarize your child with sheets of blank paper and the wonder that an empty sketch pad can provide.

Have *you* ever tried drawing with crayons? Honestly, other than the fun of the nostalgia factor, they're not easy to use unless you're two years old, and then you just want to eat them. Instead of asking Leonardo to paint the *Mona Lisa* with a broom, invest in a few quality colored pencils from a real arts store. Your youngster may discover hitherto unknown talents, through the mere fact of finally using the appropriate tools for the job.

If your children have learned the joy of reading and the value of solitary play at home, you will be able to take them anywhere in the world by simply bringing along a small bag of colored pencils, a book or two, and a sketch pad. They will have at their disposal the tools to help them sit still in comfortable silence for as long as you need them to.

Amazingly, when the time came for our return plane, four days later, an eerie sound greeted us as we entered the airport lounge.

"Daddy! Daddy! Daddy! Daddy! Daddy! Daddy! Daddy! DaddyDaddyDaddy! Daddy! Daddy, look, Daddy!" We heard the familiar, persistent whine. We could not believe our ears.

Mommy had entirely washed her hands of her young whiner, and looked as if she was plotting a quick divorce and a subsequent life in pleasant tropical surroundings. Daddy, still in his sweats and backward baseball cap, was now the designated carrier, and looked as if he could have used a quick lobotomy in the men's room. Because they had been seated behind my husband on our previous flight, it seemed only fair that the happy family ended up in front of my two boys and me on the way home.

The odious boy-child stood on a parental lap and stared back at us over the seat through much of the return trip, unnerving my five-year-old. His icy stare was peppered with occasional bursts of "Mommy! Mommy! Mommy! Daddy has a hat!" or

"Mommy, look, Mommy! Daddy's SLEEPING!" or "Mommy, Mommy! Mommy, that lady looks mean!" Occasionally the brittle shell of a mommy would glance back and vaguely apologize, telling us how much her son liked "big boys."

I wonder if he was at all curious about "big boys" who spend three-hour flights reading books and playing with magnetic chessboards. Perhaps he was inspired. Possibly it planted a seed in his tiny, desperate mind. One can only hope.

My husband, chuckling softly, periodically checked on us from his spot several seats away, and by the time we had landed and were on our way to the baggage claim, my boys were both coming up with variations on the "Mommy Mommy Daddy Daddy" theme. Like "Mommy! Mommy! Mommy, look, Mommy! I HAVE A NOSE!" from my ten-year-old, which was very rude, but funny at the time. We expected to get home and find these people on our front porch, as the sound of "Mommy! Mommy! Mommy!" seemed to dog our steps, but we managed a clean getaway.

Much is made of squalling infants on airplanes, but a crying baby pales in comparison to an annoying child whose parents haven't a clue as to what to do. Avoid this slow and painful descent into parental hell by teaching your children how to take care of themselves. By helping your child become more independent, you will help the whole family run that much more smoothly, and long waits and airplane rides will be that much more pleasant—for you and everyone else.

CHAPTER 15

THE THEME-PARK VACATION:
A LAST RESORT

I WILL GO OUT ON A LIMB AND SUGGEST THAT MOST ADULTS would not, if asked, choose as their ideal vacation destination a sweltering, overrun theme park, a place where one must navigate through crowds of screaming youngsters and hawkers of cheap collectibles. Yet due to an astonishing trend among many parents to plan their family vacations entirely around their children, otherwise reasonable grown-ups end up in exactly those kinds of places, often wearing unfortunate headgear.

Why, why punish yourself with an all-inclusive package to a hellhole that was devised primarily as an entertainment haven for thousands of children? What kind of sadistic grown-up thought this would be a fun vacation option?

It may be true that those days are gone when you could stick a pin in a map, grab some flip-flops and a fishing hat, throw a duffel in the back seat, and peel off into the sunset, but that is no reason to head for Adventure World or Fishland at the first sign of a four-day weekend. Traveling with children is challenge enough. Your reward for undertaking such a venture should be more than an overpriced walk down miles of shadeless blacktop so that you can stand in line for an hour each time you want to purchase a bag of sodden chips or watch your child ride on Mr. Vomit's Krazy Koaster.

I know, the theme-park vacation seems like an easy option. It seems easy because the rides and the restaurants and the fun are all together in one happy place. But before you fork over a pile of hard-earned currency to some perky adolescent in an orange polyester uniform, really think about the kind of vacation you would like, not the one you think will be "easier," or the one you assume your children will prefer.

It's not just to the sweltering theme parks that certain misguided adults are flocking. Certain child-friendly conglomerates now offer prepackaged "family cruises," so parents can pretend they are yachting in the Caribbean, while the children are taken into a large play area for what I can only surmise is an early indoctrination into the corporate mind-set.

Of course, it is utterly forgivable that you wish to eat and drink yourself into a sugar-and-alcohol haze while the children are being entertained elsewhere—anywhere, somewhere, just out of your sight. After doing hard time in the parenting trenches, you want nothing more than to lounge on the deck of a bright, shiny cruise ship, wearing rodent ears and mainlining a steady parade of mai tais. But it's the drinking you really want, not the fake West Indian restaurant with crew members dressed in pirate costumes. Your child may end up with a vague sense of having had fun, but this is not the kind of adventure of which cherished memories are made.

Think of the memories you and your child will be looking back on in ten or fifteen years. Will the recollection of getting a pat on the head from a stuffed corporate logo become part of the lore of her childhood, or will the legend of Mom and Dad getting everyone lost trying to find the Aquatic Oddities Museum? Do you think she will regale her own children with stories of how, when she was ten, she saw a grown man dressed up as a Power Ranger, or of how, when she was ten, she saw a hundred shooting stars in a mountain sky?

Alas, much to our chagrin, we realize that we are not always as in control of our lives as we would like to believe. Sometimes, when sharing a house with another adult and one or more children, we find that we must *compromise*. We must make *concessions*. Why, I do not know, because we are the ones who usually have the best ideas, but there you go. Sometimes Mommy has to buckle. If you do find yourself—having acquiesced to various family interests—in the middle of a so-called amusement park, there are a few sanity-saving maneuvers that might help you survive the ordeal.

If you are forced to go to one of the really popular theme parks, go on a weekday, preferably between Thanksgiving and Christmas. Super Bowl day used to be the best time to go, until about two hundred and fifty thousand people suddenly woke up to the fact that Super Bowl day would be the best time to go, and now it's the usual five-hour wait for a two-minute ride.

Get a few inexpensive disposable cameras for your kids, with the directive that they only take pictures of people sporting hats, or plaid, or mustaches. They can capture some of the more surreal moments, like the bride and groom who sat in the romantic faux-darkness of a certain faux–New Orleans restaurant, planning either their rosy future together or which rides they would be going on next. I knew they were a bride and groom because she had on a white dress and a long white veil, attached to, yes, a pair of mouse ears.

As long as you're there, you might as well enjoy yourself. Don't fight it. Give in! Breathe in the happy gas, relax, and accept the fact that resistance is futile. Arrive at your theme-park destination as if you are five years old and ready for magic. Buy funny hats for everyone, and have them monogrammed with funny nicknames. If you don't have nicknames, it's time to make some up. Eat something that makes your lips and tongue bright blue! Go on your favorite rides five times in a row! Embrace the irritation; enjoy the heat and the hordes of overfed pink people who are, unfortunately, wearing shorts. If you can manage to have fun, it will make a bigger impression on your children than all the manufactured gaiety in the world, especially if you are not normally the expansive type.

If all else fails, bring a flask! Adding a fine vodka to your juice box helps cut the sugar and imparts a general feeling of well-being when faced with giant, walking plush toys, dancing bears, and talking cartoon figures, apparitions that can be a little unnerving when you've been maneuvering around them in a state of sobriety.

CHAPTER 16

STAYING WITH FRIENDS ABROAD: DISASTER OR ENRICHING CULTURAL EXPERIENCE?

IF YOU ARE LUCKY ENOUGH TO HAVE FRIENDS WHO HAVE wisely settled in faraway and attractive ports and who are nice enough to want to welcome you into their homes for weeks on end, by all means take advantage of the opportunity. It's a wonderful experience for the children to get a taste of foreign cultures. They might come to more fully appreciate what they have at home, or they might decide that they prefer the life of a rugged Australian sailor or a pubkeeper in a small English village. And unlike a hotel experience, it is usually more interesting to see how other people live than to see how they vacation.

Let's face it: Many of us find the cost of traveling prohibitive, and the only way we can possibly ever visit faraway places is to sponge off friends who live there. Don't think of yourselves as moochers; think of yourselves as itinerant characters in a Noël Coward play—a grand family down on its luck, going for a long, long visit to someone's country estate. Make

sure your children behave impeccably at all times, which can be a challenge but is well worth the money you'll save on hotel rooms.

It can also be challenging to visit a family who might not be as close-knit as your own. You might be staying with old friends in, say, London who insist on taking you out to see the sights, and on showing you their favorite spots. It all seems like a perfect situation, until you realize that this old friend of yours and his lovely British wife bicker endlessly, every minute of the day, making each other's lives, and yours, a living hell. And you are staying in their spare room. For two weeks.

Your friend snaps at his wife and anyone else who might look vaguely happy, while at the same time planning fun things for all of you to do. His wife, who snaps right back at her husband, is put out when you decide to make life easier for everyone by devising plans that don't include them. The tension is as thick as English custard, and everyone becomes testy, except your children, who thankfully don't notice the friction, possibly because these people fight in beautifully clipped accents, which sound very *Masterpiece Theatre* and civilized. Your children have a wonderful time boating on the Thames with other tourists and marveling over the inordinately expensive sandwiches at the local coffeehouses.

Then you're off to a brief stay in Amsterdam with your friend who is recovering from an unhappy divorce. You are

whom we were fond. If we had a little crush on someone, we could take the opportunity to write an impassioned love poem, which we would leave (unsigned) in their desk, and then sigh all day, imagining the object of our affection as they opened it up after second period. If you were in third grade and mortified by the idea of saying hello to the cute redhead for whom you secretly longed, you had one day on which it was acceptable to declare your affection by writing "Be Mine," or "Please Be My Valentine," or a poem, perhaps one that began with "Roses are red," or some variation thereof. The girls always made valentines for their best girlfriends, because that's what was done, and everyone usually brought valentines for their teachers, but there was a certain frisson in the air, a certain thrilling level of anticipation, wondering if a certain someone might slip a valentine into your desk.

Somewhere along the way, some well-meaning busybody decided that too many children would have their feelings hurt if they did not get a valentine, so all emotion was excised from this formerly charming holiday. Children now pass out "valentines" to every classmate in an organized fashion, and everyone counts their candy.

True, someone might not get as many valentines as someone else—the short unibrowed girl with the saddle oxfords and bowl cut (hi!) might not get quite as many as the tall blonde with freckles. But she might get one, and it would mean more to her than if she got twenty preprinted, store-bought senti-ments. If it's too painful to celebrate Valentine's Day at school, then get rid of it. Valentine's Day has become some kind of weird egalitarian Friendship and Candy Day, so why not just celebrate "Friendship Day," or "Good Friends with Bad Candy Day"? It makes a lot more sense, since Valentine's Day has been denuded of all meaning.

For grown-ups it has become something worse, as now, apparently, the depth of our love can only be measured by how much money we have spent on our loved one's Valentine's Day present.

Valentine's Day is being marketed to a ridiculous degree, especially considering that it's a holiday that, for the most part, used to be about homemade last-minute valentines, badly cut-out hearts with hand-scrawled names and sentiments. I loved those crooked hand-drawn hearts so much that I make my child construct his own valentines, with a bunch of col-ored pencils and homemade paper hearts. Sure, his little hand cramps after writing "Be My Valentine" on twenty lopsided hearts; that's why I give him the option of writing valentines to just the girls in his class. He usually makes them for the boys, too, but at least he thinks about each person he's decorating a card for. Yes, I realize I've just admitted to homemade val-entines, and now you'll suspect me of spending my weekends busy with decoupage projects, and making decorative pencil holders out of cardboard toilet-paper tubes, and I will have lost all credibility.

But homemade cards always mean more to the recipient, and the skill of making them will last your child a lifetime of birthdays and holidays. Best of all, you can enlist your kids to make cards for you, whenever you have occasion to give one.

It is quite satisfying to be able to make a gift for someone, and a flair for homemade cards means that even if your child is dead broke she can still give someone a nice remembrance for a special day.

CHAPTER 23

YOUR VERY SUPERVISED HALLOWEEN: TALES FROM THE CRIB

THERE'S A HALLOWEEN TREND THAT I AM NOTICING MORE and more often, whereby parents and their kids now go down to the local costume superstore and buy an entire "Elvis" costume, or a complete "gypsy" or "pirate" outfit. Has everyone forgotten that you can put on one of Mom's old blouses, make a pirate's hook out of a coat hanger, slap on a homemade eye patch and kerchief, and say "Aarrgh"? You have to spend money on a scary ghost costume because a torn sheet splattered with fake blood is somehow too complicated to construct?

I am not saying you need to go all Martha Stewart on me and spend two weeks hand-sewing a complete Arthurian ensemble, with hand-carved jousting stick and homemade chain mail assembled from copper wire and gum wrappers. But why do so many parents these days feel the need to buy into the store-bought prepackaged holiday, whether it's Halloween, Valentine's Day, or Christmas?

You can avoid the big-box-store packaged costumes. Take a deep breath and exercise that imagination of yours. Suggest that your child wear a scary ghost or monster costume, because Halloween is supposed to be a scary holiday, after all—although there might be nothing scarier than a seven-year-old dressed up as a hooker. This will give you some flexibility in the event that you cannot come up with any costume at all; a little black eyeliner smudged under the eyes, some white powder, a streak of red lipstick trickling like blood from the corner of the mouth, and voilà! Night of the Living Toddler!

The sad truth, however, is that Halloween will never be what it once was. Today's parents wouldn't think of sending their children off by themselves into the night, as we used to be ushered off after dinner, armed with nothing but empty pillowcases and warnings about razor blades hiding in apples. There will never again be unattended, costumed children roaming the streets in the dark, but that's exactly what Halloween used to be.

On Halloween night, on the city block where I grew up, the only children who were supervised were the Kootes girls. They would ring the bell sometime around five-thirty, when most of us hadn't even started dinner and parents were still having their cocktails. It wasn't just the ridiculously early hour, but the fact that they were trick-or-treating accompanied by their *maid*. My friends and I didn't have maids, and to be trick-or-treating with one's maid was to be just begging for ridicule. The trick-or-treating with the maid would have been bad enough, but these hapless girls would show up in matching ensembles from Austria or Holland, starched costumes that their daddy had no doubt bought on a European business trip. The poor Kootes girls and their horrible, perfect costumes were the objects of much derision. They looked as if their mother had dressed them, and what was weirder, they were over the age of four and yet made the rounds with an adult escort. By the time our haphazardly costumed, motley group rang the Kootes' doorbell and yelled out "Trick or treat," the Kootes girls (having bathed!) would answer the door politely in their *nightgowns*. Oh, the degradation. I remember being vaguely fascinated that girls who were older than I, who were already dressed for bed at seven-thirty on Halloween night, were giving *me* candy.

A few hours later, when the girls were no doubt tucked into their downy beds, we'd begin the annual "Ringing of the Kootes Doorbell and Subsequent Running Away." We rang the doorbell and ran, only because it tormented Mr. Kootes, who hated us with a blinding, unfathomable loathing, and would chase us, fruitlessly. I don't think we thought of him as anybody's father, but our Halloween "trick" captured the true spirit of the holiday. Sorry, Mr. Kootes!

In these modern times, it seems all parents escort their children on Halloween night so they can supervise their trick-or-treating. They understandably supervised their children when they were toddlers, and when they were five years old, and so these parents continue, even when their children are eleven or twelve. Perhaps their children are entirely unfamiliar with their own neighborhoods, since they are driven everywhere by their parents. But most of these parents do not let their children play on a sidewalk in broad daylight without adult supervision, for fear they will be snatched up by the hordes of pedophile murderers who roam our streets; they certainly aren't about to start letting them out unescorted on Halloween.

At the risk of sounding like one of those curmudgeonly elders who constantly bemoan the fact that things aren't what they used to be, I nonetheless bemoan the fact that Halloween has been given over to the grown-ups. I hate that parents drive their kids out of their own neighborhoods to other areas where the trick-or-treating is better, where the fetchingly costumed kids can collect as much booty as possible before they are piled into the car and driven to another hot Halloween spot. I suppose these parents have no choice, because too many neighborhoods these days don't have a cohesive, neighbor-hoody Halloween feel on Halloween night. Neighbors turn their porch lights out and hide in dark back rooms for fear that packs of costumed teens will T.P. their houses. So of course parents search out the neighborhoods with the biggest decorations, the most fake cobwebs on the front bushes, the most elaborate cardboard headstones on the front lawn.

I suppose it's part of the natural evolution of the holidays, but every Halloween I see decorated houses that rival Santa's Village at Christmas. One house had three giant TV screens mounted above the front door, showing horror films on a continual loop; costumed actors jumped out at trick-or-treating children as they stared at the screens—a nice touch. But perhaps the scariest thing of all was the three uniformed, beefy bodyguards standing sentry at the front door. Long lines of children were quickly ushered through to dutifully receive their piece of candy, as if on some sort of assembly line. Crowds of daddies admired the high-tech flat-screen TVs and estimated the cost of the production. And this was just one tricked-out house in the neighborhood. After a few more decorated houses were admired and candy retrieved, the children were packed into cars, which then screeched off in search of their next location.

I understand that the world is a different place, and that parents are skittish about sending their children off into the scary night, their peripheral vision compromised by a rubber mask. But here's an idea: If you must drive to a more suitable trick-or-treating location, find a group of kids and their parents to join your children and you. Pick an area of, say, one or two blocks and drop the kids off in a group, at the beginning of the agreed-upon route. The parents can meet up with them at the end of the two blocks, and the children will have at least been given the illusion of independence for those two blocks. If you are lucky enough to be able to make your rounds locally, invite over some friends who don't have Halloween-friendly neighborhoods. Keep the parents together, let the kids have their own stretch of unsupervised trick-or-treating, and meet back at your place for a good old-fashioned candy count and gorge.

Suh-weet!

CHAPTER 24

CHRISTMAS COMES
BUT TWICE THIS YEAR!

THERE ARE MANY REASONS WHY PARENTS GO OVERBOARD during the holidays. Sometimes, much like those sleeping-pill aficionados who unwittingly go on midnight driving or eating sprees, they just get caught up in the frenzy and don't realize what they have done until the smoke has cleared, the credit card bills come due, and they're looking at an empty bag of hamburger buns.

For instance, quite a few of my friends who are in interfaith marriages celebrate Christmas and Hanukkah with equal enthusiasm. The more the merrier, except that their children all get a full complement of presents for both holidays.

Now, I am a big believer in presents, especially when they're for me. Presents are a wonderful part of our own holiday celebration, but they're not the only part. Though my children are half-Jewish (the half that loves lox and bagels, good chicken soup, and chopped liver), I would feel like a hypocrite if I suddenly dragged out the menorah and added eight nights of gift giving to our holiday season. Didn't people used to have to choose between Hanukkah and Christmas? And more important, where are these people putting all that stuff?

I always thought that on the first night of Hanukkah, children would receive a small token—a tiny rubber ball, perhaps, or a pair of socks, or some chewing gum. These days, a "small" gift might mean a three-hundred-dollar iPod or a palm-sized digital camera.

I realize that with the advent of tiny, expensive electronic devices, you can break the bank without even noticing that you have any extra stuff, but I see children of very tender years being given two-hundred-dollar MP3 players, along with the usual giant plush toys, manicure sets, fur coats, televisions, and laptop computers. Even I don't get all that stuff, and I'm a grown-up. Traditions are important, and perhaps you're establishing your own family tradition of celebrating our nation's rampant consumerism and runaway debt.

At the risk of sounding like a Pollyanna, I must say that it really is the thought that counts. Even if you're not in danger of being in debt up to your eyeballs after the holiday season, that's still no reason to spend hundreds and hundreds of dollars on presents for your children. If you overdo it when they're very young, you will feel obligated to top yourself each year, and then where will you be by the time they are teenagers?

If you refuse to get rid of the TV altogether, at least declare a moratorium on TV watching in the months leading up to the holidays. The voices in the TV won't be telling your children about all the merchandise they should immediately acquire, and your children won't be demanding the tonnage of marketed toys and games that will mostly end up in a pile in the corner.

There is an old cliché about children having more fun with the box in which a gift was wrapped than the gift itself; quaint, perhaps, but absolutely true. For instance, last Christmas, as I was about to throw several sheets of bubble wrap into the recycling bin, I thought about how much inexplicable joy can be had from a little bubble wrap. Being on a tight budget and in serious need of "filler" for under the Christmas tree, I wrapped up the bubble wrap in some Christmassy paper and tied it with a big ribbon. It was giant, puffy, and mysterious, and sure enough, one of the biggest hits of Christmas morning. My oldest son carefully divided it up with his brother, and the ensuing melee of unbridled glee as they popped, stomped, and otherwise mutilated their bubble wrap was a sight (and sound) to behold. Bubble wrap! It needs no batteries, it requires no reading of instructions or frustrating assemblage, and it provides immediate gratification. What could be more fun?

If you have wisely instilled a love of books in your kids, go to new and secondhand bookstores, and buy an enormous bag of books. There is something very exciting about receiving a giant bag full of books, and your child will probably not even notice if they're a little dog-eared.

Why not start a completely novel tradition next year? Take a deep breath, put your credit cards away, and buck the holiday spending trend. Spend less money, and put more thought into your gifts. Give yourself a reasonable dollar limit for each family member, and stick to it. Supplement with homemade coupons good for services (foot rub, slave for a day) or special treats (pancakes for dinner, Banana-Split Saturday) that can be redeemed throughout the year. This also sets a good example for children (who are generally not flush with cash) of how they can give a gift to a friend or a hardworking parent while on a limited budget.

And divorced parents, might we attempt to come together for the good of the children? Try not to overwhelm your kids at holiday time in your bid to outdo each other. Yes, we know you can afford a bigger and shinier and more expensive piece of equipment than your ex-spouse, but it really just looks like you're showing off, and it won't actually make your child love you more. Twice as many presents are not twice as good for your child. You will end up with tons of extra stuff at both houses, and your child will have so many things that the value of everything will become meaningless.

Christmas has gone so far over the top that I believe there is finally the beginning of a tiny backlash. The house lit up like a Christmas carnival and the holiday music blaring from loudspeakers day and night, the forced merriment and requisite frenzied gift-giving have just become too depressing for many people, and a handful of them are saying, "You know what? I'm not doing that. I'm not buying that shiny, overpriced Christmas package; I'm going to spend the holiday in front of the fireplace with my family, playing Monopoly." Try it! Toast marshmallows, make some figgy pudding, learn every verse of "The Twelve Days of Christmas." Celebrate Hanukkah in a similarly tranquil, low-budget way. It's ever so relaxing, and you'll save scads of money, too.

Now, at the risk of sounding far too multiculturally all-inclusive and politically correct, I wish you a very Merry Holiday, whatever you may celebrate. And a very Happy New Year!

CHAPTER 25

IN SANTA WE TRUST

A MOMMY FRIEND OF MINE, AS HER DAUGHTER GREW FROM baby to toddler, began connecting more deeply with the religion she had grown up with, and before long I found myself standing next to her on Friday nights, with a dish towel on my head, while she recited Sabbath prayers over some candles. (Apparently one has to cover one's head, and the Elvis dish towel was the only thing I could usually find in a pinch.)

I am not religious myself, but I'm all for anyone believing whatever they want to believe, as long as they don't try to pass laws about it, or attempt to rework my child's science curriculum. I won't try to convince you that I have fairies in my garden if you don't try to convince me that there's a kindly bearded man in the sky who doesn't want gay people to get married.

I celebrate Christmas not as a religious holiday but as a cultural one—sort of a festive pagan tree celebration, full of good food and making merry with friends. Santa, being a good pagan, is of course included in our celebration. It's about traditions. We read Christmas stories by Dylan Thomas and

Truman Capote and Dickens, eat standing rib roast and English trifle, and drink copious amounts of Christmas spirits. You're right, I'm sure Jesus didn't drink rum punch at Christmas. But I think everyone gets to celebrate Christmas in his or her own way.

And so there we were, the Christmas holidays upon us, and my friend, having discovered her own heritage and religion, started *dissing Santa Claus*. Santa Claus! Because she had reconnected to her own Santaless religion, she felt it her duty to report to her daughter, and any child within earshot, that Santa Claus did not exist. As if.

Luckily, my son wasn't much of a listener at four years old, but the point is, my friend felt I was lying to my child and that it was her duty to set all of us straight. I thought it would be impolite to point out that no one has actually seen a radio wave, either, but people believe they exist. I don't go around pulling small children into dark corners and hissing at them, "There is no God!" and I hope people would have the same kind of consideration for those of us who take Santa on the same kind of faith.

If you are not a believer, I beg you to instruct your child on the importance of sensitivity to this issue. If my own child should find occasion to let loose a loud "Jeezus Christ!" I'd tell him to keep that expression to himself, as it might offend polite company. Please tell your offspring to keep any "information" he thinks he might have about Santa firmly under his hat, so as not to ruin it for the rest of us.

So let's say you've successfully indoctrinated your son or daughter into the magical world where Santa comes down the chimney every year on Christmas Eve, miraculously navigates the hot coals that are often left smoldering in the fireplace, places small gifts in hanging stockings and under the tree, eats his cookies, downs his snifter of single-malt scotch, and hightails it to the next house. Santa has reached a level of reality where your child is now corresponding with the corpulent man in red at least once a year and generally behaving on the "nice" rather than the "naughty" side, in hopes of having a few Christmas wishes granted.

But what about when you're away from home during the holidays—how will Santa know where to go? How do you explain to your five-year-old that Santa *will* find you at that condo you've rented in Mexico for Christmas, or at the motel where you are all getting together for a large family reunion?

Plant a few seeds in your child's mind ahead of time: Steer him toward requesting small, easily packable gifts, if possible, and make sure that when he writes to Santa, he mentions where he'll be on Christmas Eve. If you will be somewhere that has no chimney—a condo, apartment, or motel room—you might share with your child that in Holland, they leave their shoes outside on Christmas Eve, and instead of coming down the chimney, Santa just walks up to the front door and puts stuff in their shoes. To be on the safe side, leave a pair of shoes by the door as they do in Holland, or outside on the windowsill, as in Iceland. In France there is some kind of Christmas Fairy who comes in through the window—presumably while Santa's catching a few winks in the sleigh—so if it's not too cold, leave a window open a crack, just in case.

Santa might "mistakenly" leave a few things back at your house, to be opened upon your return, especially something unwieldy that cannot be packed in a small suitcase. Santa might then leave a little note for your child (along with a few of the smaller presents), expressing his dismay at having accidentally dropped a few of his gifts at your child's house or apartment.

A few years back, we were meeting up in Palm Desert for a giant family reunion. It was the first big Santa year for my youngest, and he was a little concerned about being in the middle of the desert over the Christmas holidays. We were making do with the tiny fake Christmas trees thoughtfully placed in our motel rooms, and the twinkly lights festooning the potted palms out by the pool, but on Christmas Eve, we had help from an unexpected source: the manager of the motel walked by my four-year-old and casually told him that Santa was, at that moment, flying somewhere over Mongolia. Intrigued, we followed him to the motel office, where on the computer screen appeared the official site for the North American Aerospace Defense Command (NORAD), a U.S.-Canadian governmental organization ("Deter. Detect. Defend.") that runs its own official Santa tracking system, plotting the sleigh's course as it leaves the North Pole and makes its way around the world. This wonderful motel manager checked in with us throughout the evening, letting us know when Santa was spotted over Paris and England, and when he was heading over the Atlantic.

The official Santa tracking site, corroborated by grown men who were not members of our immediate family, greatly impressed my son, and being away from home at Christmas became a little more acceptable.

And by the way, a few years after her midlife religious conversion, my anti-Santa friend got divorced and subsequently married a person who not only resembles Santa Claus, but also is a true believer in all things Santa. My friend has embraced Santa with the fervor of the newly converted. She has become a born-again Santaist. Christmas is now celebrated with plastic reindeer and any number of illuminated life-sized Santa Clauses who dance the twist and make tinny ho-ho-ing noises when plugged in. Definitely a sign that Santa moves in mysterious ways.

CHAPTER 26

THE HOLIDAY NEWSLETTER: NO, I REALLY DON'T WANT TO KNOW!

EVERY YEAR I GET A PICTURE OF YOUR CHILD AND HIS DOG, or of your two children, all scrubbed and shiny and inexplicably dressed in velvet. And plaid. Plaid Christmas vests, plaid pants, fetching plaid bow ties. Sometimes the whole family is posed in a well-appointed drawing room with a Christmas tree, along with the inevitable plaid.

Why the plaid? What is with the plaid? Does any child ever, seriously, wear a plaid vest and matching pants, except on the cover of your Christmas card? Combing his hair with water and dressing him up in tartan will not disguise the fact that your child is an unrepentant bully. And telling us all about his scholastic exploits and Little League victories in your annual newsletter won't gloss over the fact that he's so unpleasant to be around, we don't ever get together with you people anymore.

The holiday newsletter is the ultimate example of parents in denial. What possesses people to put fingers to keyboard, year after year, and proceed to share far too much information

about themselves with their friends and acquaintances? What makes them think we want to know intimate details about their children's scholarly enterprises, or their own medical conditions? Yet we find these things in our mailboxes every holiday, and always from people one would rather not know quite so much about. We never get colorful yearly commentary from the truly interesting among our acquaintances; no, they are too busy living their exciting lives of work and travel and sparkling parties. But every holiday season, we receive the parade of exhaustive confessionals—everything from cheery embellishments to outright lies from friends and relatives alike.

"Scotty and I climbed to the top of the peak and made love under the stars" is an actual quote from a *real* newsletter from a *real* person. You just can't make that sort of thing up. (To save these people embarrassment, I changed his name. It's really Cliff, which, strangely, does sound made up.) I have read the intimate details of a person's liver condition, and of her husband's hospitalization. Details that, in times past, would have been saved for a very personal letter to a close friend or relative, not put on the copy machine and mailed off to a hundred friends and co-workers. Think about where all that personal information might end up. Do you really want the extensive details of your divorce and your child's academic performance to be scattered on somebody's kitchen table, for anyone to pick up and read, and possibly make fun of? Do you really want to run the risk that your holiday newsletter will be read aloud for entertainment at someone's holiday dinner party? Do you really think it's good form to tell the world that your twelve-year-old is an Olympic-caliber swimmer who just got accepted at an expensive private school and is in line for a MacArthur genius grant, even if he is? His grandparents will be so pleased, but perhaps not the friend with whom you attended college, whose own child struggles with simple arithmetic, addiction, and poor haircuts.

How about, next year, a nice seasonal card? Include a snapshot of the family, perhaps, or a stenciled Yuletide scene. There is really no need to say a thing, except "Merry Christmas!" or "Happy Hanukkah!" or "Season's Greetings!" If I need to know much more than that, I'll look for a nice long letter in the mail. And unless you're actually Scottish and want to celebrate the family tartan, ditch the matching red plaid vests. Step away from the plaid. Trust me on this.

CHAPTER 27

COCKTAIL PARTIES:
ACTUALLY FOR GROWN-UPS!

THE HOLIDAY SEASON IS A WONDERFUL TIME TO CELEBRATE with the whole family. Your social calendar becomes chock-full of turkey feasts, tree-trimming parties, latke bashes, Christmas soirees, and Hanukkah celebrations. The children eat loads of sweets and stay up late with friends and cousins. But occasionally I'll be invited to a grown-up cocktail party, for which I will happily find a babysitter or make other child-care arrangements.

We all look forward to the occasional respite from caring for children at parties: no little mouths to worry about feeding, no adult conversations interrupted by needy tots, no worries about children staying up too late, your arms free to sip cocktails and eat grown-up food.

But if you decide to throw a cocktail party for your adult friends, whether it's the holiday season or any season, here's a respectful suggestion: Perhaps you shouldn't keep your little sweet'ums up quite so late past his bedtime to attend your grown-up party. Your friends did not come over to make merry with your five-year-old, as sophisticated as she may be. They might be looking forward to some grown-up conversation, and might not feel as if they can speak with total abandon in front of a precocious tot. There is something very disconcerting about being in the midst of a heated or colorful conversation with another grown-up and suddenly becoming acutely aware of the presence of a small third party. A tiny face, staring at you intently and watching every sip you take, every canapé you nibble. Words must be censored. Behavior must be monitored.

Your friends would probably prefer not to be rounded up and herded into the playroom, so that we all might witness the impromptu musicale your bossy seven-year-old insists we all watch that minute. Nor would it necessarily be a delight to have darling Bradley climbing on our laps so that he can snatch the chips off our plates and double-dip the guacamole. You might be surprised to know that I have seen many towers built by many children with many, many blocks. It is a sheer delight to watch the blocks come tumbling down, again and again. But I would prefer to not have to watch that particular enchanting spectacle in the middle of a grown-up cocktail party.

Grown-up parties should be for, yes, grown-ups. Children should be off in the other room, sleeping or playing quietly, occasionally tiptoeing to the top of the steps and peering through the railing in order to catch a glimpse of the colorful cocktail dresses and hear the festive tinkling of glasses. Later, in the time-honored tradition, they may sneak down and steal the vermouth-soaked olives out of finished martinis, before heading back to bed. It is good for them to hear the sound of grown-ups enjoying themselves, so that they will have something to look forward to when they are older. I know you don't want your little darlings to miss out on one single bit of fun, but if your children are involved in every one of your activities, there will be no mystery to, or anticipation of, becoming a grown-up.

We all differ in what we think of as "cute," but an adult party is neither the time nor the place to display your progeny's various talents. Perhaps you might consider throwing a little recital just after the holidays, when I am going to be, sadly, out of town.

If your children are able to masterfully pass plates of hors d'oeuvres or trays of cocktails at the beginning of the evening, by all means let them make the rounds in order to greet, and subsequently extend a polite "Good night" to, the assembled guests. We will think it's adorable and civilized. Some of us may even say we want the children to stay on and enjoy the party, but we won't really mean it. Persephone's a little doll, and so is Master Ned. Now, don't they have someplace to go? May I suggest, to bed?

WHY AM I A GROWN-UP?

IT'S A WONDERFUL IDEA TO GET THE CHILDREN AWAY FROM home, to ferry them thousands and thousands of miles from all that is familiar, to introduce them to foreign foods and interesting people with charming accents. Surely it will broaden their horizons, and open their TV-glazed eyes to the magical world around them. Perhaps, you think, they will gain some perspective on how other people live, and a newfound respect, kindness, and wisdom will replace their relentless whining, petulance, and general surliness. Of course, you can travel to the ends of the earth, but if young Maggie and darling Joshua behave in the same hair-raising manner that they do at home, your trip will be nothing but a joyless round of forced marches to museums and sullen hotel-room standoffs.

In addition, inflicting your ill-behaved progeny on the unsuspecting habitants of far-off ports will do nothing to further the cause of world peace and our country's already fragile reputation on foreign soil; it might be wise to work on a few of your children's more glaring etiquette problems before leaving town.

We may worry about the state of the planet, but perhaps we should worry as well about the children we are unleashing upon it. Think of your offspring as your own little global climate zones, and deal with their unfettered brattiness before the polar icecaps of your sanity begin a permanent meltdown. Do not let loose a spoiled, arrogant child upon a world that is in enough trouble as it is, or we are surely doomed.

When you finally do get away, take the kind of holiday you will enjoy, whether it's five miles away from home or five thousand. It is not a requirement of parenthood that you vacation only in places you think the kids will "have fun." You really don't want to spend your entire holiday with the kind of people with whom you really don't want to spend your entire holiday, and I bet your children don't either. Those packaged, kid-friendly vacations might seem easier, but it would be a shame to miss out on the frogs in the shower of that lakeside cabin. You might never get to see the little house made entirely out of cola bottles, or meet that charming toothless gentleman in the desert who will fix your broken fan belt. Your car might never get stuck in the sand, and you'd miss sleeping on the roof rack, which is really much more fun than it sounds.

Getting your children out into the world they will eventually inhabit will ultimately be more fascinating to them than some wallet-siphoning kidcentric entertainment venue. Bon voyage!

Go chill the glasses. It's grown-up time.